Practical Steps to Financial **Freedom** and **Independence**

YOUR ROAD MAP TO EXITING THE RAT RACE AND LIVING YOUR DREAMS

By Usiere Uko

This publication is designed to provide competent and reliable information regarding the subject matter covered. However, it is sold with the understanding that the author and publisher are not engaged in rendering legal, financial, or other professional service. Laws and practices often vary from country to country and if legal advice or other expert assistance is required, the services of a competent professional should be sought. The author and publisher specifically disclaim any liability that is incurred from the use or application of the contents of this book.

ISBN: 147006832X
ISBN-13: 9781470068325

CreateSpace Publishing
345 Boren Ave N.
Seattle, WA 98109
Printed in the United States of America.

Contents

ACKNOWLEDGEMENTS

Success is not a solo effort. I owe a debt of thanks to so many, listing them would require a chapter of its own. I am grateful to the joy of my life, my wife Joy, for her support, long suffering, and encouragement as I marooned myself to write; and to my son Joshua and daughter Danielle, who encouraged me by believing in me, looking up to me, and starting book projects of their own. I call them "The Writers."

My thanks also goes to Ayo Arowolo, who mentored me, showed me what is possible, and read through my work three times; my brother Ndaeyo Uko, who inspired and guided me; Emmanuel Akpata, Lawal Lukeman, Anka Amurawaiye, Olufemi Oladipupo, and many others who gave input and feedback; friends and colleagues who encouraged me to go for it; and the folks at CreateSpace who made this book see the light of day.

Thank you.

INTRODUCTION

A MATTER OF CHOICE

Financial freedom is within the reach of every single one of us. All it requires is focus, persistence, and a strong desire to invest in yourself and become who you ought to be. In order to achieve what you have not achieved before, you need to become who you have not been before. It all comes down to a matter of choice.

Each time money comes into your hands, you have a unique opportunity to make a choice—to build assets or accumulate liabilities, to remain poor and middle class or to become rich. Your current financial state is a result of what you did with money in times past. You are writing the script for your financial future with what you do with your income today. Are you becoming richer or are you stuck in one spot?

Attaining financial freedom has nothing to do with how much income you receive. It has a lot to do with what you do with your current income. To change your financial future, you have to change your personal philosophy. Your actions flow from your thoughts, so you have to think differently. When this change on the inside happens, the doing part becomes easy. You first have to be so you can do in order to have. Be... Do... Have.

You can attain financial freedom starting with your current income by making a few adjustments in your personal philosophy. You'll be amazed by what a difference these few

1

changes will make in the course of your life. These simple steps, if diligently applied, will change your life forever:

1. **Make Up Your Mind.** Move from interest to commitment, from *should* to *must*. Be willing to pay the price no matter what. Cross the line and burn your bridges.
2. **Change Your Mind-set.** Upgrade from your poverty mentality to an abundance mentality. Dismantle self-imposed limitations. Think *assets* rather than *liabilities*.
3. **Know Your Financial Health.** Put your financial house in order. Know what you own, what you owe, and your net worth, assets, and liabilities.
4. **Set Clear Financial Goals.** Decide where you want to be financially in a year, five years, and ten years from now.
5. **Get Out of Bad Debt.** Shake off the yoke of consumer debt and focus on building assets rather than liabilities.
6. **Spend Below Your Income.** Cut your coat according to your cloth, not your size. Eliminate wasteful spending.
7. **Pay Yourself First.** Save first and spend what's left rather than spending first and save what's left—if anything.
8. **Avoid Budget-Busting Monsters.** Avoid the temptation to misappropriate funds. Stick to your plan.
9. **Invest in Your Financial Education.** Invest in knowledge. Know what you're doing before you jump in.
10. **Let Your Assets Buy Your Luxuries.** Don't use your income to acquire luxuries. Create assets that will generate cash flow to pay for them.
11. **Mind Your Business.** Take charge of your financial destiny. Don't depend on your employer or someone else to do it for you.
12. **Make Your Talent Pay.** Develop your talents, gifts, and hobbies and turn them into a business.

13. Develop Multiple Streams of Income. Don't depend on your salary alone. Have other sources of income.

14. Take Baby Steps. Start right where you are. Don't wait for tomorrow.

15. Insure Your Assets. Protect yourself and your assets in case of the unexpected. Don't leave your assets naked and exposed.

16. Understand Asset Allocation. Have financial security and growth plans in place before you attempt to be rich.

17. Plan Your Estate. Determine what will happen to your estate when you're gone. Don't leave it to predators.

18. Give Back to Society. Make your unique contribution and leave the world better than it was when you met it.

These steps are transformational. It's not simply a formula to get rich but a means of becoming rich on the inside through thinking rich thoughts so you can take rich actions and ultimately live your dreams in reality. The most rewarding aspect of your journey to financial freedom will not be the money you make but the person you become in the process. It's about becoming who you were born to be so you can do what you were born to do and make your unique contribution to the world.

There's no one way to financial freedom. You have to chart your individual path to your dreams. Each of us is unique, with a unique set of circumstances, talents, skills, temperament, hopes, and dreams. There is no one else on this planet like you. You alone know who you are, where you came from, and where you're heading. You are the only one who can find your way home.

This book is only a map showing you the terrain. You have to decide the specific path to take to get to your desired destination.

1

MAKE UP YOUR MIND

*Until one is committed, there is hesitancy, the
chance to draw back. Concerning all acts of initiative
(and creation), there is one elementary truth that
ignorance of which kills countless ideas and splendid
plans: that the moment one definitely commits oneself,
then Providence moves too.*

—WILLIAM HUTCHINSON MURRAY

I will never forget July 2002. I still remember the exact spot on
which I stood one Sunday afternoon after a church service at
Freedom's Ark in the northern London borough of Haringey.
My mind was troubled. Three days earlier I had received a
summons from my employer to head back to Nigeria immediately for a new assignment. My pastor asked me what my plans
were. I told him.

"You mean you're leaving your pregnant wife behind with
people you hardly know and returning alone to Lagos?" he asked

I nodded.

"I don't think you know what you're doing." He shook his head in disapproval.

I was still staring at him speechlessly as his car pulled up. He waved as he got into the car with his family. They zoomed off and suddenly I felt cold inside—and angry.

I had come to London eighteen months earlier for a project that was to last for four years. I had settled down and was getting ready to start a family when I'd gotten this mail from my employer out of the blue. Suddenly I was without income in a foreign country. My wife was a few months away from delivering our long-awaited first child. She was under consultant care due to earlier complications with the pregnancy, so I could not take her back with me to Lagos. That was out of the question. Nor could I stay behind with her. I needed my job. I ought to have quit right then, but I could not afford to. I couldn't imagine life without a salary and was too scared even to entertain such a thought. I was not a free man. I had no choice but to bow to the wishes of my employers.

In my wife's state, I could not leave her all alone in our flat, and I could no longer afford the rent. So I arranged for her to move in with a couple from church. A range of emotions coursed through my body. I felt naked and alone. I was angry. I was mad. I was powerless. I knew my wife understood, but it did not make me feel better. I felt sorry for myself.

I held back tears as I looked up at the clear London sky. Never again, I vowed, would my employer—or anyone for that matter—dictate to me how to live my life. I would achieve financial freedom whatever it took. I would live on my own terms. I would go for my dreams. If others could do it, so could I.

• • •

Deep down we all truly desire to live life on our own terms—to do what we want how we want and when we want it. To live our dreams. As children we believed anything was possible. We lived in a make-believe world where dreams always came true. When we grew up, we were made to believe life doesn't work that way. We had to stop dreaming and start earning a living. Building castles in the air will not put food on the table, which you have to do before indulging in the luxury of dreaming about your future. You have to retire before you go for your dreams.

The fact that most of us have given up on our dreams doesn't mean that dreams don't come true. The fact that your clock has stopped working doesn't mean that time has come to a standstill. Dreams come true; it just hasn't happened to you yet. We watch it happen to others. We see it on TV, where every day people like you and me start ordinarily and achieve extraordinary things. We call them *celebrities* and queue up to collect their autographs.

If others can do it, why can't you?

What do they have that you don't?

What do they know that you don't?

Good questions. You may have made various attempts that took you nowhere. Your New Year's resolutions may have ended in a puff of smoke. You may have concluded your parents and other naysayers were right after all. Maybe it was not meant to be. There's nothing special about you. Your past defines your future and ultimately your destiny. Don't bother trying. Who do you think you are? Quit dreaming and face reality.

Nothing can be further from the truth. You have all it takes—if you're willing to pay the price. Anyone who is willing can have whatever he wants. The trigger point is when you make up your mind to go for it whatever it takes.

However, making a decision is not enough. The quality of the decision is the deciding factor. You'll be tested by trials, storms, and setbacks. If your decision isn't firm, you'll turn back and give up. Until you fully commit to the decision, you have not made up your mind.

For most of us, making up our minds is a process. We can make a decision to go for it today, falter tomorrow, turn back the day after, and make another attempt weeks or months later. You have to make up your mind until your mind is fully made up. That's when you move from interest to total commitment. That is when you cross the point of no return.

MAKE A ONE HUNDRED PERCENT COMMITMENT

Your mind is fully made up when you get to the place of one hundred percent commitment. Talk is over. Internal debates come to an end. No more excuses. You move from should to MUST. You throw your hat into the ring. You're ready to put your money where your mouth is. If you falter you'll push on regardless. You're ready to pay the price. You've burned your bridges

Getting to the point of one hundred percent is the most difficult step for most of us. There are differences between desire, interest, and commitment, although they all look alike. With desire and interest, there's a chance of turning back. With commitment going back is foreclosed. It's like water: at 211 degrees it's scalding; at 212 degrees it boils. That's the tipping point. Anything short of 212 degrees is just not enough.

It's the same with one hundred percent commitment. Until you get to that point, there's a chance of drawing back. Whenever difficulties show up, we grab that chance and throw in the towel. We've all been there, cruising on New Year's Resolutions Boulevard. We reel out lofty goals on January 1 and get on our way merrily but begin to run out of steam around Valentine's Day. We give up and return to our old routine.

The best way to avoid this trap is to make a firm decision to follow through to the finish line. The moment you are one hundred percent committed, there's no chance to draw back. Your mind is made up and you don't have to think about the issue again. Case closed. No retreat, no surrender. There's no room for going back to debate it: Shall I? Shall I not? Maybe. You've made up your mind to give it what it takes. You will accept no excuses whatsoever.

This frees up tons of energy that would otherwise be expended on internal debate on the topic over and over again, robbing you of crucial energy to create the momentum to move forward. It frees you to focus fully on the task at hand. This is what separates winners from losers: one hundred percent commitment.

So how do you get to the point where your mind is fully made up?

What makes you to get from the point of desire and interest to the point of commitment?

What takes you to the tipping point?

WHEN ENOUGH IS ENOUGH

Change happens when you get to the point of enough. You've suffered enough, endured enough pain, abuse, and shame, received enough, learned enough, understood enough, attained enough awareness, and, if you're like me, talked about it enough. Enough is the tipping point. A day comes when something snaps inside and you know—this is it. The cup becomes full and runs over. For some it can happen in an instant, but for many it takes time.

When there's still more room to endure, you continue to tolerate. You're not there yet. You continue to murmur, complain, and wish. But the moment you've had enough, you act decisively. You rise up and just do it. You change habits, laws, government, pursuit of a goal, etc. You walk away from an abusive relationship, a job you hate, a neighborhood you dislike.

Take, for example, Mohamed Al Bouazizi. Tuesday, December 17, 2010 was a day like any other day in Sidi Bouzid, the small town in Tunisia where he lived. Mohamed was a young college graduate turned fruit vendor, and one morning he went out to ply his trade. In a routine confrontation, municipal officers seized his fruits for lack of legal permit and when he protested, he received a beating. He went to the municipal building to demand his property back and received further beating. He then went to the governor's office and demanded an audience but was refused.

Something snapped. Mohamed had enough. He decided his voice must be heard no matter what. With all doors slammed in his face, he drenched himself in paint thinner and set himself ablaze. That fire ignited a revolution that is currently raging through the Arab world, sweeping away heads of state in its wake. When the history of the Arab Spring is told, Mohammed's name will be written in gold as the tragic hero who started it all.

Enough is where the trigger is. More often than not, anger plays a crucial role, as in Mohammed's case. Anger often brings out the boldness you lack in your more sober moments. Anytime I feel really angry, I channel my anger at the root cause of the problem to ensure it does not happen again. Some of my streams of income came to me out of my anger at not having enough money. Rather than dissipating that anger in endless arguments with my spouse, I vented my frustration on my projects. This served me well in moving them off the drawing board into reality.

Many entrepreneurs ventured into the business world out of anger. They hated their jobs, what their bosses did to them, or being fired for no just cause. After endless searches for other jobs, the anger built up to the point where they decided to take the bull by the horns and go for it.

Enough is where full commitment occurs and change happens. This explains why when fifty people attend a seminar, forty-five jump and scream, "Aha!" but one year later only ten people have walked their talk. The remaining thirty-five still have some distance to go before they get to enough or reach their tipping points. They still need an extra push to get there.

You need to keep going until you get to the point of one hundred percent commitment to going for your financial freedom dreams—until you've learned enough to attain the comfort level you need to commence your journey. You have to keep pushing yourself until you get to your tipping point. Deep down in the soul of every man and woman is a yearning for greatness and attainment of their utmost potential, but often the price to be paid keeps us stuck in our comfort zones. The pain of not living your dreams is waiting further down road, so you have to pay either way—now or later. It's better to embrace the pain of discipline for growth than face the pain of broken dreams and an unfulfilled life.

DEFINING MOMENT

The commitment to go for it is the force that will propel you through the steps, decisions, and processes that will transition you from the old to the new. Life is about making decisions, and some decisions change the course of your life for good. These are called *defining moments*. Life is made of many of them. Deciding to go for your financial freedom is one. The journey changes your life for good. As you proceed, you gain clarity of your purpose, grow as a person, become richer, and become free to live your dreams.

MY STORY

I still remember Christmas 2001 as if it were yesterday. A member of our charity group, Haringey Peace Alliance, had invited my wife and me to dinner to celebrate a successful rally we'd just held in Northern London against drugs, crime, and gangs wars. As the evening wore on, the conversation shifted to the Oprah Winfrey show and one interesting guest: Robert Kiyosaki, author of the book *Rich Dad, Poor Dad*. I had missed the episode because I was at work and couldn't contribute to the conversation—and I seemed to be the only one. But I was intrigued by what I heard. Poor Dad sounded very much like my real dad.

Something inside told me I needed to read that book. I ordered it from Amazon the moment I got home. When it arrived and I turned to the first page, I couldn't put it down until I got to the last chapter. I had last read a book in 1989, when I'd left the university. Now I was possessed.

Because of this book, I became aware for the first time that I was heading nowhere and history was about to repeat itself. I was a Poor Dad waiting to happen. I was walking the path of my father. I knew deep down this was not where I wanted to end up. Like Robert I have a huge respect for my father—who, incidentally, was a teacher like Robert's dad. I had thought that studying engineering would give me the clean break from the past I desperately needed. I was dismayed to find I was still stuck in the rat race, armed with an engineering degree and working for an oil company.

What did I have to do to escape?

Desperate for answers I ordered the second book in the Rich Dad series—*Cashflow Quadrant*. It increased my awareness and made me see things in a whole new light. It awakened my desire for learning. I laid my hands on any book I could find on financial freedom and personal finance. I became a reader. By the time my employers ordered me to pack my bags and return to Lagos, I already had a plan and turned the anger into a propelling force to execute it. I would start an Internet business and use the cash flow as a buffer while I returned to my first love: writing. This time, though, rather than write fiction I would reach out to those who were still trapped like me and let them know they had a choice. I would write about freedom.

• • •

When you're fully committed, heaven moves and things begin to fall into place. Until your mind is made up, you cannot take the right actions on a sustainable basis. The journey to financial freedom is not a walk in the park. There are no shortcuts. If you believe the hype about attaining financial freedom in three months, you'll believe anything. You need to grow as a person in order to witness growth in other areas of your life. It's not about a formula to get rich quick. It involves unlearning some of the beliefs you hold dear—beliefs that produced the results you're currently unhappy with. Beliefs that have left you trapped in the rat race.

You will be required to take some bold and courageous steps. One is taking responsibility for where you are right now and bringing the blame game to an end. The moment you take responsibility for your present, you are ready to take responsibility for your future. This is a defining moment.

FAILING FORWARD

The fear of failure and rejection is one of the main obstacles to making up your mind. Memories of past failed attempts tend to make us conclude we cannot move past this point unless something extraordinary or supernatural happens. Consequently we give up rather than learn the lessons from our last attempt and give it another shot.

Failure is actually part of the process. It comes with the package. It's an integral part of success. It gives us time to pause, make course corrections, and proceed. You will fail on your way to succeeding. It's simply a matter of time. But the best lessons are learned when things go wrong and you have to fix them. When we succeed we tend to party but when we fail we ponder. Failure is simply feedback letting you know you're not doing something right. It's a call to make adjustments so you can go further. You don't succeed by never falling but by rising each time you fall.

If you're afraid to fail, you're not ready to succeed. Failure is a true test of commitment. If you're not one hundred per-cent committed, you'll be tempted to pull back at the first sign of failure, when the going gets tough. And if you're afraid of failure, you're afraid of success. Failure is a stepping-stone to success. It's part of the package. The will to learn the lessons from failure and push on regardless of difficulties and setbacks is what distinguishes winners from quitters.

Most of us have been brought up to be afraid of failure. This holds you back from stepping forward. Failure is not an enemy but a teacher. You may not like its manner of approach, but never lose its lessons. It shows you what works and what does not, what to throw away and what to keep. It shows you the true colors of those around you—those who truly believe in your vision and those who are in it for what they can get.

Failure also reveals your true character, whether you're a learner or a blamer. It tests your commitment to the goal.

Failure should be expected and provided for in your plan. Some call it plan B, a safety net, or "what if?" What if things do not go as planned? What do you do? You may need to allow it more time, have a cash reserve, try another approach, get a job, or hold on longer to your job, depending on what the goal is. When a nurse is about to give you an injection, she'll warn you it will hurt a bit. If you jump up and run out of the hospital, you're in effect saying you're willing to live with the ailment rather than take the jab, endure the temporary discomfort, and get well. Likewise if you avoid failure, which is a temporary setback, you're kissing success goodbye. You have to take the shot or forever wonder what might have been.

There are two ways to respond to failure: learn or blame. How you respond determines how far you go. If you don't learn the lessons, you cannot progress to the next level. All you have left are excuses.

EXCUSES 'R' US

Excuses come in very handy when we want to avoid responsibility for outcomes. Rather than make up our minds and make it work, we shop for reasons why it will not work. Excuses are two a penny, buy one get one free. The moment you consider the option of not doing something, excuses come easy. The moment you contemplate the possibility of backing off from a commitment, you mind comes up with just enough reasons to back up that decision.

Until our minds are made up, we are ready to entertain excuses. Old, limiting mind-sets provide us with the excuses we need to remain immobilized in the prison of our comfort zone rather than step forward to embrace possibilities and our dreams.

We wait for our dreams to happen rather than make them happen.

We wait for circumstances to change rather than create the circumstances we desire.

We wait for the ball to come to us rather than reaching out for it.

One of the paradoxes of faith is man's waiting for God to move while God is waiting for man to move. Man ends up blaming God when nothing moves.

STEP OUT OF YOUR COMFORT ZONE

If you want to change the results you're getting, you have to change what you're doing. There's security and comfort in old habits and status quo. And if you've been in jail for a long time, freedom is a scary proposition. You're so used to being fed and catered to that you begin to doubt your ability to fend for yourself in the outside world.

It's the same with employees. It's much easier to live paycheck to paycheck, accumulating liabilities rather than building assets, minding your business, and ultimately living your dreams. You're scared stiff of life without your salary. You end up believing that living your dreams is not possible. You believe you're not cut out for it. All you can look forward to is your retirement, hoping your pension and retirement savings will still be there to support you through old age.

Stepping out of the prison of your comfort zone can be a daunting task if you allow fear to hold you bound. We tend to forget that we overcame obstacles to get to where we are today. If you can come this far, then you can go much farther. All you have to do is to step out yet again.

You have to come to the understanding that the person you admire so much was like you once upon a time. Chances are you're better off than he was when he started out. If he can make it, you stand a better chance. Despise not your days of small beginnings. Do not look down on yourself. You can make it. You have what it takes. You may have issues with commitment, but the moment you clear the hump you'll be well on your way. Believe you can. Don't shoot yourself in the foot.

It's never too late to start taking full responsibility for your financial future. You have to decide to end the blame game. You have to accept full responsibility for your past financial misdeeds and commit to taking the steering wheel of your financial affairs and financial future going forward. You have to make the switch from being reactive to being proactive; you must learn rather than blame. You have to take responsibility for your finances rather than depend on others to do it for you.

GOODBYE, YESTERDAY

To embrace the future you desire, you have to say goodbye to your past. Forgive your parents, teachers, uncles, and aunts for giving you the impression that the world of abundance is beyond your reach, that all you need to do is go to school, get good grades, get a good job, climb the career ladder, and save for retirement. Forgive yourself for the dumb financial decisions you made in the past, for having little to show for the quantum of cash that has passed through your hands all these years, for acquiring liabilities and thinking they were assets. Forgive all who cheated you or borrowed and have not paid back, making you lose faith in the human race. Forget about your past financial setbacks and move on.

Take a deep breath and let it go. Let go of the past and the baggage that goes with it. You have held onto it long enough, and it has slowed you down to a crawl. You may have lost a lot of time, but it's not too late to start anew. Wipe away that tear and say goodbye. Your best days are still ahead.

IN SUMMARY

To embark on the journey to financial freedom on a sustainable basis, you need to come to the place of one hundred percent commitment. The manner of getting there differs based on what works best for you. The fact that you made a previous attempt and failed does not mean you should give up altogether.

- Make up your mind to take charge of your financial affairs. Turn your murmuring and complaining into commitment to action.
- Start learning instead of blaming. Learn from your mistakes and fail forward. Don't give up.
- Keep making up your mind until your mind is fully made up. Continuous learning can aid this process—learning until you're ready to commit fully. Pain and anger can also help in taking you to the place of full commitment
- Forget about the past. Do not allow what happened in the past define what you think you're capable of.

2

CHANGE YOUR MIND-SET

As a man thinks in his heart, so is he.
—PROVERBS 23:7, HOLY BIBLE, KJV

Your journey to financial freedom does not start with the state of your finances or bank account but in your mind.

Your mind-set controls your thoughts.

Your thoughts influence your actions.

Your actions determine your results.

Consequently your mind-set determines your results.

You are where you are right now as a direct result of your past mind-set. The decisions you made in the past produced the present you are experiencing today.

To change your results, you have to change your actions.

To change your actions, you have to change your thoughts.

To change your thoughts, you have to change your mind-set.

Ultimately your mind-set determines your present and future. To change your future, you have to change your mind-set.

According to Webster's dictionary:

> **Mind-set:** *a mental attitude or inclination. 2: a fixed state of mind*

Your mental attitude or inclination influences your thoughts the way the course of a river influences how the water flows. To act differently you have to think differently. Making the switch from lack to abundance principally involves changing from a lack mind-set to an abundance mind-set, from being passive about your finances to taking control actively. Abundance does not fall from the sky. You have to create the channels required for it to flow toward you.

The mind-set that got you to where you are now cannot get you to where you desire to be. A lack mind-set cannot create an abundant reality. Taking the right actions with the wrong mind-set is a recipe for failure. Your mind-set will sabotage your efforts and steal the wind from your sails. This is the reason why formulas by themselves do not work. There must be an alignment or congruence between the mental and physical for sustainable results to happen. There must be unity of purpose or integrity (oneness). You have to change your mind-set to align with your actions in order to arrive at the desired destination.

To influence your output, you need to take control of the input. You have to start taking full responsibility for where you are right now rather than blaming external factors. If you do not take responsibility for the present, you cannot take responsibility for the future. It's as simple as that.

When you come to the realization that your actions or inactions created your today, you are in a position to create the tomorrow of your dreams by acting in alignment with your desired future. As stated in the previous chapter, you have to move from waiting for things to happen to making things happen, from being reactive to being proactive. You have to switch from giving excuses to taking action. The best way to predict the future is to make it happen. One sure sign that you have made the switch is realizing that you can get what you want if you're ready and willing to pay the price of thinking and acting in alignment with what you really want.

ECHOES FROM THE PAST

Your current mind-set and money reflex have their roots in your upbringing and your past experiences with money. We do not learn money management skills in school. Money does not come with a user's manual. You can have a PhD and work for a college dropout, living from paycheck to paycheck.

Our primary money lessons and skills are learned at home, from how our parents handled money and what they said about it. For example:

Money does not grow on trees.
I am not made of money.
I did not pick the money from the floor.
Don't build castles in the air.
Daydreaming does not put food on the table.
Growing up, the most common word you probably heard was *no*, especially when it came to money. We were made to believe we couldn't have it all.
No, you can't have that.
No, don't touch that.

No, you can't go there.
No, we can't afford that.
No, you cannot always have what you want.
No, everything is not about you. Think of your siblings.
No, no, no.

These lessons have been reinforced along the way by your early experiences with money, your thoughts and feelings toward money, and your current reality when it comes to money. It has become a self-fulfilling prophecy perpetuated from generation to generation. You grow up thinking that abundance is off limits for everyday folks.

Hence the universal mind-set toward money is one of scarcity and shortage. The belief is that there is not enough money to go around. For me to have more, you have to make do with less. We are taught in school that resources are limited and human needs are insatiable. We have come to believe that financial freedom and abundance is a fantasy that exists only in the world of celebrities, a mirage that moves away as you move closer. For the rest of us, all we can do is try to make ends meet. Most believe the proverbial ends will never meet. Expenses will always be a step ahead of income. It's a lost battle.

The cycle of life is to be born, go to school, get good grades, land a safe and secure job, climb the ladder as far up as you can, retire, wait for your pensions, try your hand in a business or two, and wait for your turn to answer the final curtain call. End of story. This is the belief most of us have. This is the reality we know. We have seen this played out before us with our parents, uncles, aunts, senior colleagues, etc. That is life as we know it. It's our fate, our destiny.

This gives rise to negative, disempowering thoughts like:

I will never be rich.
It takes money to make money.
I will retire and live on my meager pension.
There is no rich person in my family, hence I can't be rich.
Starting a business is too risky. My friends tried and failed.
No business can give me returns equal to my salary.
A bird in hand is worth two in the bush.
Investing is risky.
I cannot take risks.
It's better to be safe than sorry.
The economy is down. I cannot make it in business.
The banks are not giving loans anymore.
I am not business inclined. I come from working-class family.
I don't have what it takes to make a lot of money.
I am not good with money.
I don't have what it takes to run a successful business.
I am not smart enough.
I am not good enough.
I am not a lucky person.

The list is endless. You can throw in a couple of yours for good measure. Our minds have been bombarded by poverty and limiting thoughts for so long we have come to believe a lie and it has become our reality. Our minds block out possibilities staring right at us and opportunities right under our noses. We walk right past them every day, our minds set on the next promotion at work, our next salary increase, a better job, more bonuses, or a financial miracle (an unexpected gift, an inheritance, a lottery win etc).

POVERTY IS AN INSIDE JOB

Poverty is a state of your mind, not the state of your finances. The lack you experience is the end result of poverty-inspired actions you took arising from your poverty mind-set. The battle is won and lost in the mind. A poem by C. W. Longenecker captures it beautifully:

If you think you are beaten, you are,
If you think you dare not, you don't.
If you like to win, but you think you can't,
It is almost certain you won't.
If you think you'll lose, you're lost,

For out in the world we find,
Success begins with a fellow's will.
It's all in the state of mind.

If you think you are outclassed, you are,
You've got to think high to rise,
You've got to be sure of yourself before
You can ever win a prize.

Life's battles don't always go
To the stronger or faster man.
But soon or late the man who wins,
Is the man who thinks he can.

Poverty mentality and thoughts lead to poverty-producing actions. Poverty is an inside job and has nothing to do with your income or the cards life dealt you. A high income does not automatically translate to wealth. It's not how much you earn that determines how rich you become; it's what you do with how much you earn.

A poverty mind-set can convert high income into a mountain of liabilities. Poverty mentality is the root of most financial crimes. More financial crimes are committed in the high-income bracket than in the low-income bracket per capita. Many have wrecked their careers and reputations. Some have landed in jail.

What you believe is real becomes your reality. Scarcity is self-made. There are sufficient resources on the planet for everyone to have more than enough. You attract what you believe. You become what you think about most of the time. Your capacity to receive is determined by your mind-set.

You can create wealth. You can choose to create new markets rather than fight for a share of an existing market. Sony created most of their products first before creating a market for them. A perfect example is the Walkman. There was no market for it. Sony created the market. Apple too created products before consumers realized they need them. The possibilities are limitless when you make up your mind that a new reality exists. You're no longer limited by what you see with your physical eyes but by your imagination.

You get what you ask for. Ask, you shall receive; seek, you will find; knock, the door shall be opened unto you. What you have depends on the size of the container with which you approached the ocean of abundance. The size of that container is not determined by your academic IQ or special abilities but the boundaries you created in your mind as defined by your mind-set.

WE CHOOSE WHAT WE SEE

The eye sees hundreds of thousands of images a day. What registers in your awareness is based on what you consider important, what you focus on, what you look out for. Changing your mind-set also means changing what you focus on, what you look for, what you see, and ultimately what you believe. What you seek, you find. It is with the mind that you see. Hence you choose what you see.

If your mind is somewhere else, you can walk right past something without becoming aware of it. If you find yourself very hungry in a neighborhood you have never been in before, every restaurant will jump out at you. If you're looking to buy flowers, you will not miss the florist. If you're looking for women, you will see them even while driving with one hand and talking on the phone with the other. You cannot take in everything you see at a glance. You have to choose what you see.

Have you noticed that the moment you make up your mind to buy a certain model of automobile, you begin to see that model almost everywhere you go? Before then you hardly noticed. So where did they spring out from?

The fact is they have been passing you all the time. You took no particular notice because your mind was not on the lookout for them. It was not on your watch list. This phenomenon is known as your *reticular activating system* (RAS). It makes you notice things or resources that were always there but were previously unnoticed. The moment you determine you want something and focus on it, you brain places it on its watch list and brings it to your awareness anytime you come across it. Hence it doesn't matter whether you're consciously on the lookout for that car or rushing to get to an appointment; anytime that model comes into your field of view, it will jump at you. Same with when you're looking for your name on a big bulletin board. It jumps at you at a glance from among a sea of other names.

Opportunities can be right under your nose but unless you have them on your radar, you'll walk right by without noticing them. This includes opportunities to achieve abundance. This explains why a foreigner can come to a country and flourish while some citizens languish for what they perceive as lack of opportunities.

In every town there is the good, the bad, and the ugly. Each town has it rich and poor neighborhoods. You'll see mass housing, overflowing garbage, and people sleeping under bridges. In the same town you'll find exquisite tree-lined boulevards, clean air, and luxury automobiles. Two tourists can visit the same town and go away with two different impressions based on the aspect they focused on and the areas they visited. This also applies to lack and abundance. If you have a lack mind-set and mentality, you will see lack everywhere you go. Lack will jump out at you. You'll gloss over abundance because you feel it's not for you. When you come face to face with abundance, you'll give excuses why you cannot grab it.

WHAT DO YOU REALLY WANT?

Most people do not dare think of what they really want because they feel it's a waste of time. Remember, Momma said we should not build castles in the air. It does not put food on the table.

Changing your mind-set also involves thinking of what you really want rather than want you don't want. What you focus on manifests. We have seen that thoughts become things. When you think about something long enough, you start to take action.

Why then would you go about thinking of what you don't want?

I don't want to be poor.

I don't want to be broke.

I don't want to live in a bad neighborhood.

I don't want to drive a beat-up car.

I don't want to retire poor.

I don't want to feel tired all the time.

I don't want to work for an ungrateful boss.

I don't want…

Every day you bombard your brain with the words *poor*, *broke*, *bad neighborhood*, *beat-up car*, *tired*, *ungrateful*, etc.

When you focus on what you don't want, you get more of it. Why not bombard your brain with good and positive words? *Rich*, *abundance*, *enough*, *new car*, *big house*, *nice neighborhood*, *love*, *joy*, *passion*, *gratitude*, etc. Why not ignore what you don't want and focus on what you really do want?

For every *I don't want* there's an *I want*. Why not simply overwrite *I don't want* with *I want*?

Do you think about what you're thinking about?

Do you listen to the words you speak?

MY STORY

I used to focus on what I didn't want in my marriage, on things that were not happening and expectations that were not met. The more I looked for what was wrong, the more I found it and the more I nagged and complained. I started having constant quarrels with my wife, and she began withdrawing from me, sometimes not speaking to me for days. Things were going from bad to worse, and soon we were voicing innuendoes about regretting marrying each other.

Then a word from my pastor, Tunde Bakare, hit me like a thunderbolt:

If you change the way you look at things, the things you look at will start to change

It dawned on me that I was focusing on things to murmur and complain about. I was focusing on things I did not want. I had a word with myself. I decided to start looking for things to be grateful for and things I really wanted but already had. I started to become grateful. The more I looked, the more I found what to be grateful for.

I came upon the startling revelation that I could not have come that far in life if not for my wife. I used to think I had succeeded in spite of her. It was a very sobering thought. I had to eat humble pie and be truly thankful. My marriage was never the same again. The days of constant quarrels became a distant memory. I felt more grateful with each passing day, and the things I used to complain about became history because I decided to focus on the positive rather than the negative.

Oftentimes, when I think about my wife and my kids and how far I have come, I feel so grateful I become so overwhelmed. I have to lock myself in the bathroom and cry. I wonder why I am so blessed. My thoughts changed, my feelings changed, and my actions changed. I am now experiencing a new reality.

This realization of the impact of focus has helped me immensely in directly my focus in the direction of what I really want rather than what I don't want. Now, when I need something—say a new car—I do not tell myself "I cannot afford it." Rather I ask myself, "How can I afford it?" That puts my brain to work. Since I don't believe in using my capital to buy luxuries, I get to work thinking about how to create the asset that will pay for the car. Somewhere down the line, the answer drops into my mind. The first time I tried this I used an investment opportunity in the stock market. The second time I had my business pay for the car, and for my current car I had a new stream of income pay for it. I would not have benefited from these opportunities if I had allowed lack mentality to close my mind to the possibility of affording the car I wanted.

• • •

If you're serious about attaining financial freedom, you have to make the choice to change your mind-set. Envision abundance rather than lack. When you focus on abundance, you will begin to see it all around you. As you see it, you start to believe it. If you believe long enough, you start to speak and act in alignment with your thoughts, taking abundance-creating actions, and ultimately abundance manifests in your reality. You are what you think. Your thoughts and beliefs ultimately lead to action. When you're in the action phase, the course is set for inevitable fulfillment. It's only a matter of time.

It's easy to blame the economy, the government, our parents, our bosses, our spouses—everyone but us for our failures or lack of progress. That is a loser's mind-set. The reality is you created the lack you now experience through your thoughts and actions or inaction. When you realize the awesome power at your disposal to make things happen, you stop giving excuses for actions based on fear, laziness, and mediocrity and start taking control of your life, directing it along the path of your dreams. By taking responsibility for your present, you are in effect taking responsibility for your future.

YOU CAN CHANGE YOUR MIND-SET

Most people think we have no control over our thoughts or mind-sets. We do. You choose what you think. You create your mind-set. You are the man.

You can decide right now to think about your childhood home, your junior high school, an old friend, or a family reunion. You can play back the images and experience the feelings associated with them one more time. You can also choose when to bring your thoughts to the present. You can entertain thoughts and you can push thoughts away from your mind. You are in charge.

If you allow your thoughts to roam free, you have decided by your inaction not to take action. You made that choice by default. You cannot blame anyone for what's going on in your mind. No one can force thoughts on you, even in communist China or North Korea. Your thoughts are all yours. You own the copyrights.

Your mind-set is not cast in concrete. You can choose to think differently. You have the power to change your mind-set in an instant or over time. This usually happens when the truth hits home—sometimes like a bolt of lightning, making you aware of the damage you've caused through wrong thinking. It's a matter or reprogramming or thinking differently until new thought patterns are formed to replace the old. With a new worldview come new thoughts, new information, new beliefs, and new paradigms. When you realize you have the wrong map, you need to get a new one. A wrong map will land you in the wrong destination no matter how far or fast you run.

You can change. You can choose to control and focus your thoughts rather than allow them to roam free like a butterfly, flitting from one subject to the other without focus and concentration. Self-discipline starts with controlling your thoughts and focusing it in the direction you desire.

Your thoughts control your feelings. When you control your thoughts, you control your feelings. The way you think about someone determines the way you feel about that person. You can no longer blame your feelings. You create them through your thoughts. A good way to know what's going on in your mind is to watch your feelings. If you have bad feelings, you're thinking bad thoughts. If you feel good, you're thinking good thoughts.

This control is critical, because without control you cannot determine outcomes. You're like a passenger in a car, at the mercy of the driver. If he makes a dumb mistake, you pay for it, sometimes dearly. Similarly you can choose to act to change your feelings rather than wait for your feelings to change so you can act. You can change your circumstances rather than wait for circumstances to change. Be like the thermostat, which determines the temperature—not the thermometer that simply records it.

CREATING A NEW MIND-SET

Creating a new mind-set involves a shift in paradigms—the glasses through which we view the world. The easiest way to achieve this is through personal growth and development.

The following steps will get you well on your way:

- Develop a reading culture. Read autobiographies of your role models, personal development books, and books on personal finance, motivation, and inspiration. Invest in books that will change your life.
- Listen to audio programs and watch DVDs on personal growth and development, improved performance, goal

setting, success principles, time and life management. Listen to audio tapes of your favorite motivational speakers. Listen to and watch inspirational radio and TV programs. Watch life histories of successful people. Watch programs that educate, entertain, and inspire rather than endless movies, news, reality TV, sports, etc. Use your media time wisely.

- Attend seminars on areas you need to improve. Invest in your personal development more than in clothes, gizmos, or your car.
- Get a mentor who has achieved what you want to achieve and is ready to teach you.
- Choose your friends wisely. Make friends with those who are heading in the same direction as you—friends who will help you along, not pull you back or mock your dreams.
- If you can, move to a better environment that nurtures your new mind-set and inspires your dreams. If you live with your parents and have a job, you may want to get a place of your own. Expose yourself to realities other than your parents'.
- If your current job is not giving you room to grow, consider moving to another unit or looking for another job.
- Be selective about which websites you visit. Aim for those that educate, inform, and inspire rather than just news, social media, sports, etc.
- Spend your spare time wisely. Focus more on personal development than socializing and working extra hours. Use your commute and idle times productively. Minimize influences that reinforce the old mind-set.

Feed your mind and soul with positive messages and images. It bears repeating that as a man thinks, so is he. What you think of consistently manifests. Stop focusing on what you don't want and start focusing on what you really want. Change your vocabulary. Change your environment. Shut down inputs that perpetuate the old mind-set. Push out the old stuff by bringing in the new. Bombard your mind with new messages and images.

Soon you will begin to see a new world you never knew existed—and it's right next door. You couldn't see it earlier because you didn't know it existed. There's so much going on that we don't know about. You find what you seek.

MY STORY

Although I had a pastor who believed there is greatness in every man, I had no clue how to get there except through hope and prayer. Most of the stuff I heard Sunday went right over my head. I could sense my pastor's frustration. How could I be exposed to such awesome teachings but remain in status quo year after year?

He alluded that he had more to give out but sensed that we, his congregation, were not yet ready for it. While trying to figure out why we did not seem to be getting it, he made this profound statement:

"A truth declared before its time will fall on deaf ears"

I had felt that, as a Christian, if I prayed long and hard enough, in due season providence would move on my behalf, and by an extraordinary set of circumstances beyond my control my dreams would come true one day. All my troubles would be over. All my prayers would be answered.

I have since found out the hard way that hoping and praying is not enough. Faith without work is dead. After praying long and hard, I have to get to work on my goals and dreams. There is a price to pay.

Reading the book *Rich Dad, Poor Dad* opened my mind and marked not only the commencement of my journey to financial freedom but also my journey to personal growth and development. The book inspired me to start reading other books. Gradually I acquired a reading culture and started building a personal library.

I came to realize that knowing what to do was not enough. I needed the discipline, commitment, and focus to keep doing it until I got the desired results. These would come from personal growth and development. Financial education could give me wings, but personal growth and development were the wind beneath my wings. Without it, I could not fly very far.

My mind opened up as I read more books. Without realizing it I was changing from the inside. I had embarked on one of the most exciting journeys of my life. I started having goals and gained clarity on who I really was and what I really wanted. A lot of things started making sense to me, including stuff my pastor labored to teach me but sounded like a foreign language. I made the mental crossing from being an employee to becoming an entrepreneur. A whole new world opened up to me—a world where dreams do come true.

One of the things that changed when I started my own journey was a gradual shift in priorities. Before then I had principally spent my free time visiting friends and watching TV. In the 1980s and 1990s, TV stations in Nigeria were not on twenty-four hours a day. They went on around 4:00 p.m. on weekdays, midday on weekends, and went off by midnight. I knew all the programs by heart, from the children's zone to documentaries to news to soaps. I also knew how each station signed off. Most nights I would wake up past midnight on the sitting room couch to the sound of loud static on the TV as the station had gone off. I was a bona fide TV addict.

As my new mind-set kicked in, I started reading more books and watching less TV. I bought a computer and started spending more time in front of that than my in front of the TV screen. Now I hardly watch TV. I often catch up with news online. My time is so precious I think twice before making time commitments. Back then my personal rate was $0 per hour. Now my time has value both immediate and residual. The assets I now use my time to create will continue making money long after I have stopped working.

With my new mind-set, I had seen and started to experience a new world that's alien to most. If I could make the crossing, I believe, anybody can. I had everything possible stacked against me, including a bad case of low self-esteem, a huge dose of cynicism, and a lack of role models. I adopted my mentors through books and took it one day at a time. I am truly amazed how far I have come—it's beyond my wildest imagination.

Along the way I raised the bar and dreamed new dreams. With the experience I've gained and, most importantly, who I have become in the process, I know I will achieve my new goals. The change I've gone through inspires me. I used to litter the landscape with abandoned projects; now I follow through. I am more in control and I create my circumstances.

I'm not telling you this to brag. I'm still a publicity-shy country boy. The only reason I'm telling my story is to let you know that if I could change, anybody can. All you need is a desire for change strong enough to make you step out of your comfort zone and go for your dreams. When your mind opens up like a flower in bloom, you will know what actions to take. No one will need to tell you. You will be in a position to take your destiny into your hands and run with it.

IN SUMMARY

Your mind-set is your most critical success factor in your journey to financial freedom. It determines how far you go. Your current mind-set cannot take you much farther than you have come. To move to the next level, you have to invest in your personal growth and development.

- Start with a book. Reading this book is a very good first step. Don't stop reading. Start with a book a month, then two books a month, then one book a week. Look at the list of recommended reading at the end of this book. Nothing opens your mind like reading a good book.
- Spend your time wisely. Go over the steps to developing a new mind-set. Cut down on TV and socializing that does not improve your quality of life or move you toward your goals.
- Choose friends wisely. Spend time with people who have the same goals as you as far as financial freedom and personal development. Get a mentor who will communicate with you in person, via phone calls, or through books.

3

KNOW YOUR FINANCIAL HEALTH

My problem lies in reconciling my gross habits with
my net income.

—ERROL FLYNN

Your next step is to come clean about your true financial state. Ignorance is not bliss. To be able to get a proper handle on your finances, you need a clear picture of your true financial position. The truth hurts, but to be able to treat a disease you need an accurate diagnosis.

The reality is that most of us don't know the true state of our finances. We don't know our numbers and we're scared of what we may find if we probe deeper. We feel if we ignore the problem, it will somehow sort itself out later when our income increases. Actually, increased income exacerbates the problem. It's like a leaky pipe: increased flow makes it worse, and ignoring it will not make it go away.

There are varied reasons why you may be clueless, ranging from laziness to fear to shame. But you know deep down something is not right, and you're afraid of what you may find if you lay all your cards on the table. Whatever the reason, you have to put away your fears and come face to face with your true financial position because what you don't know can hurt you. If you don't know how deep a hole you've dug yourself into, you may keep on digging deeper. You have to come to terms with your true financial health and deal with it. Think about:

What do you owe (debt)?
What do you own (equity)?
What's your net worth?

You need a clear snapshot of your current financial situation in order to know the magnitude of what you're dealing with. You cannot fix what you are not aware is faulty.

You owe it to yourself and your loved ones to put your finances in order now rather than later. Many people's true financial state is only known at death, when their loved ones are forced to put the pieces together to close the books and execute the estate. Sadly some still slip through the cracks due to poor record keeping. This is avoidable.

So often you hear stories of folks who lived poor and died rich. They had no clue they were worth so much because they never cared enough to find out. If they had put their financial houses in order earlier in life, they could have gained more control, deployed their assets more profitably, and lived richer and more fulfilling lives, leaving behind bigger inheritances to their loved ones. Ignorance can be very expensive.

BURIED IN CLUTTER

Financial clutter obscures the true state of your finances. It comes in different shapes and forms:

- Important documents lying around the house.
- A failure to file documents properly.
- Misplaced property title deeds, stock portfolio statements, investment papers, etc.
- Unopened bills.
- Unopened bank statements.
- Unopened letters from brokers, financial and investment advisers, etc.
- Unpaid dividend checks.
- Cash lying around the house—under sofa cushions, in shirt and trouser pockets, in car pigeonholes, in luggage compartments, in old bags and unused wallets, you name it.

Some of us don't even know where our checkbooks are. We need to turn the whole house upside down to find them. Same with other important documents.

CLEAN HOUSE

You need an urgent and massive spring cleaning of your finances, starting with de-cluttering your home and your life. Confusion obscures the true position of things and stands in the way of building new assets. It's hard to tell what's trash and what's good stuff.

You cannot spring clean your finances without doing the whole house. Old clothes and other items you no longer need have no business occupying space in your house. Sell what you can and give what you can to friends and charity, then send the rest to the trash. Too much stuff stands in the way, causing unnecessary distraction, and it's the reason you've earned so much and have precious little to show for it. Stuff saps your finances. Get rid of it. Say goodbye to the past and focus on the present and future.

De-cluttering also has a lot to do with respect. If you do not treat your money with respect, you repel it. It cannot come together and achieve something meaningful when it's lost in clutter. You need to take care of your money, nurture it, and create an enabling environment for it to grow and flourish.

Clean out your house and your life. The most effective way to go about it is to clean your house with your finances at the back of your mind. As you're dealing with stuff, put together all your cash and important documents. By the time you're done with the whole house, you'll be ready to deal with your financial affairs.

Let go of stuff you no longer use. Your home is not a museum of ancient stuff. Uproot all your documents and cash from wherever they're hiding. Go through your house from top to bottom with a fine-tooth comb, sparing nothing. As you go along, keep aside stuff that's no longer of use and needs to be shown the way out. If you have clothes you haven't worn in six months (except seasonal or special occasion clothes) or appliances you haven't used in a year, they can be considered clutter. Let them go.

Clean out your closets. Check your trouser and shirt pockets. Check under the cushions and under the couch. Sometimes things slip in the gaps in the upholstery and disappear mysteriously. Find a way to open the seams at the bottom and set the captives free. You'll be surprised by what will come crawling out—stuff you long gave up as lost like cash, documents, cutlery, remote controls.

Gather up everything you need to piece together the current state of your finances. Keep a bunch of large envelopes handy to set up a filing system when you're done.

Go through your papers. Open all your bills. Dispose of the ones that have been settled and piece together the true picture of your financial health. Sort it into two groups: what you own and what you owe.

YOUR NET WORTH

Start with what you own. You may be surprised to find you're worth much more than you thought. What property do you own? Gather the papers together. What of your stock portfolio? Call or pay a visit to your broker if need be and obtain an account statement. This will tell you how much stock you own and its current market value.

What about your bank accounts, both savings and checking, active and dormant? Put your bank documents together and sum up your account balances. Let go of accounts you no longer use. What about other money market instruments, bonds, or certificates of deposit?

Update your records with your bank, broker, and anyone you do business with. Make sure they have your correct address. A lot of bills and account statements end up in the wrong place because of a lack of current information.

What about cash on hand? Sum up all you rescued from all the unlikely places. Look around the house. What do you have of value that can be readily converted to cash if the need arises? Note this under things you own.

A useful guide is to imagine you're relocating to a foreign country and you're fully packed. How much would you get if you sold the remaining stuff? That will give you a good idea of the value of what you own. Remember you may not get more than ten percent of the purchase price if you were to sell an item at a yard sale. Also put a value on your jewelry and precious metals. Gold, silver and other precious metals often appreciate, and have going market prices per ounce. They hold value more than stuff.

Turn your pile of clutter into a pile of cash through a yard sale. For your car you can check online to get the going price for its model and year, but typically you get less when someone pays cash for it. You may want to mark that price down further by about thirty percent. That's the problem with stuff: it depreciates rapidly.

What do you owe?

What's outstanding on your mortgage, credit card, and other loans?

Go through your bills. Keep the up to date ones and trash the old. Add up all your outstanding bills and debt.

Go over what you have again to make sure you didn't miss anything major. Now subtract what you owe from what you own. The resultant figure is known as your *net worth*. Congratulations—now you know. And you may be feeling disappointed. Maybe it's not as high as you thought. At least now you know the truth. Very few people know their net worth. Some sit on a pile of cash but live poor due to ignorance. Most think they're rich while in reality they're close to bankruptcy.

There's no use hiding your head in the sand. This snapshot of your current financial status is crucial in your journey to financial freedom, as it forms the basis of your financial planning and goal setting. You have to know where you are before you can project where you can get to in the next year and beyond.

Your net worth is not a reliable figure to use in gauging your true financial state, but it's a useful guide. For instance, some of the items you listed under what you own are not really assets. Even if the prices you attached to them reflect what you would get at a yard sale, you may not get buyers. You may end up giving the items away.

Your net worth also gives you an idea of your wealth-conversion ratio—a measure of your ability to convert income to wealth, which ranges from low to medium to high. It tells you what you've been doing with the money that's passed through your hands all these years. If you quickly calculate or estimate how much you've earned since you started working and compare that to what's left now you'll get a rough idea of your ability to convert income to wealth.

What you do with your income is more important than how much you make. Knowing your financial health gives you an idea whether you've been turning cash to trash or wealth. Improving your ability to convert income to wealth is a required key to attaining financial freedom. If your wealth-conversion ratio is low, you will remain poor no matter how much you earn.

It's very easy to be lulled into believing everything is okay when you look at your big house, fleet of luxury automobiles, latest toys and gizmos, etc. Your net worth tells a better story, but in the coming chapters you'll see net worth alone is not enough. If what you own isn't generating cash flow, you're cruising in the financial slow lane.

MY STORY

I first carried out this exercise in the summer of 2003. It was my own moment of truth. The result made me very sad and mad at myself. It was glaringly apparent that I had virtually nothing to show for the first ten years of my working life.

Most of what showed up in the asset column was stuff I had retained since 2001, when I'd commenced my journey to financial freedom. When I looked at what was left of my years of hard work since I'd taken my first job as a college graduate in 1991, I felt like a complete fool. Everything I had spent money on was gone: the cars, the rent for my house, the clothes, the home appliances, furniture, everything. By 2003 I had bought a new car and changed my wardrobe, furniture, and appliances. Everything I had labored for from 1991 to 2001 was gone with the wind. All I had were memories and a plot of undeveloped property miles away from civilization.

My ability to accumulate wealth was close to zero. I suffered from acute spending disorder—an unhealthy addiction to liabilities. I was spending money on all the wrong things, stuff that was here today and gone tomorrow. I was converting cash to trash. It was a massive wake-up call. I have remained awake since then.

YOUR FINANCIAL FITNESS TEST

A financial fitness test can show in a nutshell the state of your financial health based on examining some basic financial habits. Carrying out a financial health check should not be a one-off affair but a routine exercise. I recommend you do this at the end of every quarter (four times a year). If you have financial goals, you need to check up on how you're doing. You need to know the score. Without it any game becomes an aimless rigmarole.

Taking a financial fitness test is a quick way to get a snapshot of your financial health. There are many such tests available.

The one below takes only twenty minutes. All it requires are simple yes or no answers:

1. I spend below my income. I spend a maximum of seventy percent of my income on living expenses. (Yes/No)
2. I have enough money to pay my monthly bills in full. (Yes/No)
3. I take advantage of resources available to help meet my financial goals (e.g. tax reliefs, employer matching contributions, etc.). (Yes/No)
4. I use a budget to guide my spending and savings each month. (Yes/No)
5. I have written financial goals with a date and amount (e.g. save $15,000 for a business startup by December 2012). (Yes/No)
6. I have a plan for expenses that do not occur monthly and have enough money for them when I need it. (Yes/No)
7. I have an emergency savings account with enough money to cover three to six months of my living expenses. (Yes/No)
8. I calculate my net worth (assets minus debts) at least once every year. (Yes/No)
9. I review my credit report annually. (Yes/No)
10. I use credit only to pay for assets. (Yes/No)
11. I have adequate insurance (auto, home, life, and health). (Yes/No)
12. I keep my financial records organized. (Yes/No)
13. I pay my bills on time every month. (Yes/No)
14. I balance my bank account every month. (Yes/No)
15. I save money on a regular basis for long-term financial goals (e.g. children's education, seed capital, house, retirement). (Yes/No)

THE REVIEW

If you answered yes to zero to six questions, you need help. You're on the slippery slope to bankruptcy. You need to take drastic corrective actions to get your finances back on track. More money will generate more expenses, making a bad situation worse. You need to get a good grasp of personal finance fundamentals and quickly regain control of your finances. You may need to see a financial adviser to guide you.

If you answered yes to seven to ten questions, you're headed for financial difficulty. Now is the time to take action and get financially fit. You need to put in a more conscious effort to regain control of your finances and take responsibility rather than go with the flow.

If you answered yes to eleven to thirteen questions, you're doing a fair job of managing your finances and have taken some steps in the right direction. You need to invest further in your personal financial education and financial literacy. Being in control of your finances is not the end of the story. You need to take a further step to increase your income through investing your savings.

If you answered yes more than thirteen questions, you're in good financial shape. Keep up the good work! You're a step ahead of the pack. You need to invest in your financial education and get real-life investing experience if you have not done so already. You need to keep your finances in shape and increase your income to get ahead financially. With one aspect under your belt, you're good to go for more.

KNOW YOUR FICO CREDIT SCORE

A July 2008 study by the Consumer Federation of America (CFA) shows that seventy percent of Americans don't know what constitutes a credit score and how to improve their scores. The report goes on to state that consumers could save $28 Billion a year in lower credit card finance charges if they improved credit scores by thirty points. Many people underestimate the impact their credit score has on their financial life. But this simple, three-digit number may stand between you and a car loan or home mortgage.

Your credit score, typically called a FICO score, is named after the company that developed it: Fair Isaac & Company. Your FICO score ranges from 300 to 850 and is calculated from different data in your credit report. This data is grouped into five categories and weighted as shown below:

Payment history: 35%
Amounts owed: 30%
Length of credit history: 10%
New credit: 10%
Types of credit used: 10%
For more details, check the official website:
www.myfico.com.

Lenders believe the higher your number, the better the chance you will make your loan payments on time. It's much easier for them to look at this number than go through your entire credit report to come up with their own risk evaluation. The best scores are in the 720 to 850 range while the worst scores fall in the 300 to 500 range. The higher the number, the better your score. The folks in the 720 to 850 range get the best deals when it comes to loans and financial products. With clients like this, lenders can go to bed with both eyes closed.

You have to know your financial numbers in order to gain control over your finances—and you must work at getting them to move in the direction you desire.

IN SUMMARY

> *A problem well stated is a problem half solved*
> —CHARLES F. KETTERING

Half the battle is won when you can put your finger where the problem is. So you need to know the actual state of your finances before you can do something about it. As you look at what has become of all the money that's passed through your hands, it may be easy to see you have challenges accumulating wealth. Something is wrong with the way you handle money.

In order to gain control of your money, start with the following steps:

- Plan to take one day off to clean out your home. Go through all the stuff you've accumulated but hardly use and move it out. Dispose of it.
- Piece all important documents relating to your finances together, including cash on hand, and determine what you own and what you owe.
- Dispose of what you no longer need through a yard sale
- Determine the value of what is left by imagining you're relocating to a foreign country and you're fully packed. How much would you get if you sold the remaining stuff in a yard sale? That will give you a good idea of the value of what you own.
- Determine your net worth by subtracting what you owe from what you own. Compare that with the mental figure you've been carrying around. More often than not, your net worth is much lower than you thought.

- Take the financial fitness test. Look at the results and note where you're not doing well.
- Decide you're going to close those gaps, and start finding out how. Develop a plan.

4

SET CLEAR
FINANCIAL GOALS

Without goals, and plans to reach them, you are
like a ship that has set sail with no destination.
—FITZHUGH DODSON

To achieve anything worthwhile in life, you need a goal and
a plan to achieve it. This holds true for attaining financial
freedom. You need unambiguous financial goals in your
journey to financial independence. You need a clear idea of
what you aim to achieve and when you want to achieve it so
you can track and measure your progress. You need a clear
vision of success: How will you know you have achieved it?
What does it look like, feel like, taste like? What do you
really want?

Your immediate goal should be SMART:

Specific
Measurable
Attainable

Realistic
Time-bound

Specific means it should be very clear, without any ambiguity. *Measurable* means you should be able to measure your progress and know for sure when you have achieved it. *Attainable* means it's something that is doable. If you set goals that break natural laws, you're setting yourself up for failure, e.g. attempting to become a billionaire in one year, which violates the law of gradual growth.

Realistic, in this context, refers to the timeframe for realization of the goal. Dream big, but give yourself a realistic amount of time to achieve it. Often it takes longer to attain a goal than you first thought it would.

Time-bound means you must set a timeframe for the achievement of your goal.

For example:

"I want to earn $100,000 between January 1 and December 31, 2012."

This is:

Specific: $100,000
Measurable: Dollars
Attainable: It can be done. Many have done it before.
Realistic: One year is enough if you're willing to give what it takes.
Time–Bound: January-December 31, 2012.

This is a clear financial goal. There is nothing ambiguous about it. Come December 31, 2012, all you need to do is to itemize all you earned all year and compare it to $100,000. You either met your target or you missed it. Numbers don't lie.

The beauty of a SMART goal is you don't need to wait for the end of the year to check your progress. You can do that on a monthly basis. To make it easier for you, cascade your annual goal into monthly goals. If you're starting out, your income will pick up slowly, so don't simply divide your annual goal by twelve. Start small and step up. If you miss the first month, you can consider it a lesson learned and correct your mistakes if there are any.

If your goal is in bite-size pieces, you'll find it much easier to chew. This keeps you focused, calibrates your effort, and brings you out of your current comfort zone gradually.

So, at each point in time, you need to know the score:

- Are you on track?
- Are you winning?
- Are you losing?
- Do you need to change players?
- Do you need to change tactics?
- What do you need to do to get back on track?

You have to aim for something if you want a fighting chance of achieving it. A life without goals is aimless. A journey without a destination goes nowhere. Imagine a football match without goal posts. That is anything but football.

Your financial goals determine what actions you need to take on a daily, weekly, and monthly basis. If you have no idea what the goal is, you cannot score. If you have no idea what the score is, you cannot win the game. You're in this game to win. In order to do that, you need clear goals and objectives.

Your financial goals have to be clear and precise.

When setting your overall financial goals, you need to connect with your inner desires and determine what you really want, not what you think is possible. This is to avoid selling yourself short. If your goal is based on where you are, you will not go far nor reach beyond the sky.

To move to the next level, you have to set a goal beyond your comfort zone. Your goal should stretch you. If you're comfortable with your goal, it shows you're still within your comfort zone.

Do not allow fear to shortchange you. Suspend doubt and unbelief, and really express yourself. Forget about your current reality for a moment. Break through self-imposed limits. You have to determine your long-term desired destination upfront. What is your dream? More often than not, your journey to financial freedom is the path to your dreams.

WHERE DO YOU WANT TO BE IN FIVE YEARS?

Shoot for the moon. Even if you miss, you'll land among the stars

—LES BROWN

How much annual income do you want in five years' time? This is life giving you a blank check. This is your ticket to the next level. Put down the figure. How much net worth are you looking at? Again, put down the figure. How much savings and investment? Sketch your five-year goals in figures. If you want to go into real estate, how many buildings do you want to own? Are they apartment buildings, commercial real estate, something else? What monthly cash flow will they generate? What will be the value of your asset portfolio? If you want to build a business, what turnover are you looking at in five years? How many employees? Break down your dream into facts and figures.

Right now it might look silly to you—like a childish game of make believe. As you grow as a person, you will come to realize dreams do come true and you can really write whatever you want on the blank check life gives every single one of us. One key fact you need to understand is goals put your subconscious mind to work. You may not know how or when, but the moment you commit to your goal your subconscious mind goes to work on the puzzle—and usually comes up with the solution when you least expect it. The resources you need for the journey show up when you move. This is when heaven moves too. This is where opportunity meets preparation. It starts with having a clear goal.

A PLAN IS THE BRIDGE TO YOUR DREAMS

After having a clear picture of your goal, you need to connect it to your current reality. You need a plan—a bridge to your dreams or goals. What do you want to achieve in the next one year? This brings it closer home.

Before you run with your financial goal for this year, you need a quick reality check. Cascade your annual goal to a monthly level. Let's assume, for example, your financial goal for 2012 is to save $15,000 from a net annual income (after taxes) of $30,000. This means you intend to save $1,250 per month or fifty percent of your net salary. This is a clear, unambiguous goal.

The next question is: is it doable? Say you currently save $2,000 per annum. Can you live on half your salary? Not likely. However, the strength of your desire may be such that saving $15,000 in one year is a task that must be done. Let's forget for a moment what you need the $15,000 for—a down payment on a house, to go back to school, to start a business, whatever. The most important thing is the strength of your desire. If you decide it is a must-do, then something simply has to give way.

Take a good look at your expenditure pattern and decide it's a new day. Anything you don't need to survive must be put aside this year—vacations, cable TV, eating out every week, high-street fashion, a new car, new furniture, a new TV, you name it. You do not want to live the rest of your life this way, but for the sake of this goal you must be willing to pay the price. Someone with clear financial goals cannot afford to stare too long at the Joneses and find out how much their new toys are worth. Your eye will be on your financial goals rather than how affluent you look among your peers. Don't care what your friends will say. Your vision of success must be so compelling you're willing to do whatever it takes to make it happen.

When you get to this point, you're ready to fly. The issue is not what you have to give up. The issue is that after giving up all there is to give up, you end up with $1,250 every blessed month in your bank account for the next twelve months. That's the power of having a clear financial goal.

Your financial goal may go beyond saving fifty percent of your monthly salary to developing multiple streams of income, thereby increasing your income by whatever percentage you desire. We are each unique and have unique issues, so there is no one formula that fits all. What matters most is getting to take the steps that will lead to the attainment of your financial goal.

PUT IT IN WRITING

*Write the vision, make it plain, so that he who sees
it may run with it.*
—Habakkuk 2:2 (Holy Bible)

Don't keep your financial goal in your head. Write it down. Keep it where you can see it every day: in your wallet, by your bathroom mirror, somewhere private where only you and those you want to share your goals with can see it. It is very easy to make a goal and forget all about it months later. The very act of writing down your goal sends a strong message to your subconscious mind that you are serious about it. When you see your goal every day, it helps you to maintain focus on your thoughts which ultimately results in action.

MY STORY

Prior to embarking on my journey to financial freedom, I had no financial goals. I didn't know I was supposed to have any. I had been brought up to believe money would take care of itself and I wouldn't have to worry about it. I simply had to work hard, pay my tithes, provide for my family and aged parents, and give to the needy and heaven would smile on me. I had been taught to save for a rainy day, only I couldn't keep my hands away from the money until the rain came, so I had no savings. Anytime a need or emergency cropped up, I ran to friends and family. I was taking my financial life one day at time.

Deep down I wanted to be rich and free. Although mechanical engineering paid the bills nicely, my dream was to leave the corporate world and live the life of my dreams—writing, painting, and living in a ranch far away from noise and traffic. I had no plan for how to achieve it. My expectation was that if I gave enough, God would bless me beyond my wildest imagination.

I never sat down to ponder in what form that blessing would come. I fancied someone would pull me over someday and tell me he had a message for me from God. He would lead me to the trunk of his car and hand me a fat briefcase filled with money. That was my concept of a blessing back then. If I gave away lots of money, money would come back to me a hundred and a thousand fold. All I needed to do was give, do nothing, and wait.

As I learned about setting financial goals, I started to set some for myself. As I attempted to meet them, my spending habits started to change. I saved, and I cut down on needless spending. I avoided the trap of trying to catch up with the Joneses – my fellow colleagues in the oil industry. I soon became the butt of jokes. People began to wonder what I was doing with my high income.

Gradually I started investing in the stock market—before it became fashionable—and the bulls went on a rampage. I started a business and started buying real estate. I focused on assets and multiple streams of income. Gradually my dreams started appearing doable. As I set goals and achieved them, my self-confidence soared and I started setting more audacious goals. I came to realize I was truly blessed and the blessing had not come because I had waited for someone to give me tons money. I realized as I began to discover myself and give my gifts, I started making money. I did not live in a ranch yet, but having come that far, I knew it was simply a matter of time.

IN SUMMARY
Your financial goal should be SMART:

Specific – What do you really want? State it clearly without any ambiguity.
Measurable – put the actual numbers down (dollars, units etc)
Attainable – should be in alignment with universal laws and principles.
Realistic – give yourself ample time to achieve it. It usually takes longer than you anticipated.
Time-bound – give yourself a deadline.

You need to set clear financial goals and develop a plan to achieve them. You can have what you really want if you're willing to pay the price to achieve it. Others before you who achieved and surpassed the goals you desire are mere mortals like you who started with nothing and paid the price.

No goal is unrealistic. What is unrealistic is your commitment to achieve it. It's easy to have a goal. Most people fall short when it comes to the commitment to see it through to the finish line.

- Write down your goals and make it visible so that you can run with it.
- Dream big and start small. Break down your overall goal into tasks you can achieve immediately.
- Keep track of your progress and make corrections where necessary.

5

GET OUT OF BAD DEBT

*The only man who sticks closer to you in adversity
than a friend is a creditor.*
—Author Unknown

Having clear financial goals helps you put debt in its correct perspective. In short, it restricts your cash flow, especially consumer debt like credit cards or loans. If you have bad debt in your hands, you need to get out of it fast. But first, you must understand what you're dealing with.

GOOD DEBT AND BAD DEBT

There are two types of debt: good debt and bad debt. Good debt makes you richer while bad debt makes you poorer. Good debts are incurred in acquiring assets while bad debts are incurred on liabilities.

How do you make the distinction? An asset puts money in your pocket while a liability takes money away. Look at which direction the cash is flowing. If it's going away from you, it's bad debt, and that's a liability. If you have bad debt, pay it off as soon as possible. If you delay the interest piles up and may outgrow the principal sum. Bad debts include loans for consumer items, depreciating items, and items that do not generate net-positive cash flow such as cars, furniture, and household electronics. They cost a lot, depreciate rapidly, and end up as junk eventually. At the end of the day, the item and your money is gone for good.

If the money flows toward you, that is good debt. It pays for itself and puts money in your pocket. If you have good debt someone else is repaying, with some extra coming into your pocket, you want more of that. An example of good debt is taking out a loan or mortgage on a rental property with a net-positive cash flow. If the total rent on the property covers the mortgage or loan payments, maintenance, fees, and insurance *and* puts extra cash in your pocket, the asset pays for itself. In fact it often appreciates in value and generates net-positive cash flow. The more good debts like this you have, the richer you become. You need more good debts and zero bad debts.

HOME MORTGAGE

Your home is not an asset in the world of the financially literate. Your home does not put money in your pocket. Rather it takes money away from you by way of maintenance fees, insurance, taxes, and so on. If you have two mortgages without a tenant, you may be heading for financial crisis. Taking a mortgage on a home makes sense since part of your payments will be converted to equity in the home, whereas if you're renting you have no equity in the property no matter how long you live there. In that case a mortgage makes sense financially.

However there are instances when a mortgage does not make good financial sense. A mortgage loan can come back to haunt you if property prices crash after your entry. The bank will not absorb the difference. You have to pay up. Also if you're in a town for short period of time it may be better to rent than buy.

Another danger with a mortgage is too much house. Many homebuyers have a tendency to bite off more than they can chew—especially when the bank pays for the main chunk of it. But your castle can swallow you up and you can find yourself struggling to keep up with your monthly payments, with precious little left to live on. In this instance the first thing to do is abandon your castle and run for dear life. Put your home on the market and go get a smaller one. That will free up your cash flow and allow you space to exhale.

If you can pay off your mortgage before term, by all means do. But if you fall behind in payments, the bank can repossess the house. Taking a mortgage loan on a home is not always a good idea. You have to study the market and think it through rather than follow the crowd.

BAD DEBT BAGGAGE

Bad debt pulls you in a negative direction. It's a very heavy load to carry. Bad debt weighs you down financially and emotionally, lowers your self-esteem, makes you anxious and fearful, constricts your cash flow, and renders you incapable of meeting your financial goals with respect to savings and investment. Debts to friends and family can strain relations and terminate friendships even further.

> *Before borrowing money from a friend, decide which you need most.*
> —AMERICAN PROVERB

A debtor is a slave to the creditor. When you're behind in payments, you start to avoid your creditor and if that happens to be your friend, it's even more trouble. You live under the shadow of shame and feel unnecessary pressure to tell lies and make bogus promises to get yourself out of tight corners. Overdue bad debt can make your life hell with endless phone calls, sheriffs or debt collectors, and repossessors. You cringe at the sound of the doorbell or the phone. It seems as if the whole world is out to get you.

TOMMY'S STORY

I remember the first time I met Tommy (not his real name, to protect his identity) as if it were yesterday. It was spring 2001 and Tommy was on the run. I was in Houston for a project assignment and Tommy's uncle was my neighbor. In his late twenties, Tommy had lost his job some months earlier. He could no longer afford the rent on his apartment and the minimum payments on his credit cards and fell behind in his car payments too. His had repossessors on his tail, no savings, no assets, and nothing he could fall back on. With the loss of his job, his financial world had literally fallen apart. The threat of losing his beloved automobile was the last straw for Tommy. It was all he had left to show for his years of working.

When the heat became too much, Tommy sought sanctuary at his uncle's. I met him there; he was a beaten and bitter man, full of regrets, mad at the system and the world. His uncle asked him to do the right thing and hand over the car. Tommy was very upset because he had repaid more than seventy-five percent of his loan. He fished for sympathy from me. I tried my best to get him to let it go and embrace a fresh start.

Two weeks later the repossessors were back on his tail, and Tommy was back on the run. I didn't hear from him until weeks later when he returned to his uncle's, tired, haggard, beaten, and penniless. The repossessors finally caught up with him and he lost all his money and his prized car.

• • •

It was a sad story, but it happens all the time. At the peak of the financial crisis, some vandalized their own houses in anger on their way to homelessness. They lost their homes and their equity in those homes. Middle-class folks, thrown out of their homes by creditors, had to move into tents.

PUT OUT THE FIRE

You need to relieve yourself of the bad debt burden. The first line of attack is to stop digging yourself deeper into the hole. In a pipeline fire, the first line of attack is to shut off the fuel supply. Fighting the fire while the source is feeding it constantly is waging a losing battle.

> *Today, there are three kinds of people: the haves, the have-nots, and the have-not-paid-for-what-they-haves.*
> —EARL WILSON

Stop spending. If your credit cards got you into trouble, grab a pair of scissors, cut them to pieces, and put them out of action. Use cash until you are fully out of financial rehab and can trust yourself with the deadly plastic. Is your ATM card fuelling your spending addiction? Give it the same treatment. Protect your bank account from ATM withdrawals and use the bank instead. If your account type does not allow use of the bank, change to one that does, or change banks. Make it harder to access cash. My wife Joy's formula is to go without ATM cards and use a bank with fewer branches so her savings is as far away from her as possible.

Once upon a time, there were no credit and debit cards, and we did just fine. Now it seems inconceivable that we can leave home without our beloved plastic. But you must say goodbye to them until you're out of the woods. Return to the basics and plan your cash flow. Are impulse items your weakness? Cut down your visits to the mall and only shop for essentials. Too much expensive partying? Cut down on social outings and the expenses that go with them. There are a thousand and one ways to stop the bleeding. Whichever one applies to you, do it immediately. If you do not need a thing to survive, cut it.

FACE YOUR DEBT AND DEFEAT IT

Determine your full debt exposure (covered the previous chapter) and begin to face it with courage. Do not be afraid of the mountain of debt you've racked up. Burying your head in the sand will not make it go away.

With the deadly plastic out of the way, you'll have more cash to increase your debt repayments. Do not make minimum payments, which increase your interest. Pay off your debts as quickly as you can. Meet your creditors and work out plans to repay based on your current financial circumstances. By all means deal with them with integrity and come clean if you cannot meet their terms so something can be worked out.

Tackle the debts with the highest interest rates first—typically credit cards. These debts can take on lives of their own if you make only minimum monthly payments. Your interest can overtake the principal and you may find yourself drowning in an ocean of debt. Pay them off as soon as you can.

There is a debate over whether to pay yourself or your creditors first. There is no one right answer. It depends on your particular circumstances. The ideal situation is to pay yourself first. This makes sense if your savings or investment gives you a higher return than the interest rate on your debt. Also you need money for emergencies, especially if you have a family. You cannot run on zero savings in the name of debt repayment.

You can, however, cut out the excess fat in your budget and do both: pay yourself first *and* pay down your debt. When you pay yourself first (treated in detail in Chapter 7), you generate an additional cash flow by investing your savings. This additional cash flow can help pay off your debts faster. Determine what works out best for you. Consult your financial adviser if you have one.

You cannot go on this journey with bad debt drawing you back, creditors breathing down your neck, and your mind ill at ease. You need to be fully in control of your finances to be successful. Declare a financial state of emergency if you have to. Call your family to the situation room and read them the riot act...then sound the trumpet of jubilee. The prison doors are open. It's time to be debt-free!

IN SUMMARY

Determine what type of debts you have. Good debts are debts you incur in acquiring assets. This means the asset repays the debt and puts some money in your pocket. You need more of these.

Bad debts are debts you incur in acquiring liabilities. This means you have to repay the debt by yourself. You need to get out of this position. Review your debt portfolio and take decisive action.

If you have bad debts:

- Stop spending. If your life does not depend on an item, don't buy it. Stay away from the malls unless you're buying groceries.
- If your credit cards put you into trouble, destroy the plastic and pay cash for your purchases. If you don't have the cash, don't buy it.
- Make it harder to access cash to fuel your spending habit. Rather than endless visits to the ATM, use the bank. Don't use ATM cards that draw on your savings account.
- Pay off your debt rapidly, starting with the debt with the highest interest. Do not make only minimum payments on your credit cards. Pay them off as soon as you can. You may have to make huge sacrifices to make this happen as soon as possible.

6

SPEND BELOW YOUR INCOME

There are plenty of ways to get ahead. The first is so basic I'm almost embarrassed to say it: spend less than you earn.

— PAUL CLITHEROE

The beauty of your journey to financial freedom is not just the rewards that await you on the other side but who you will become in the process. By changing your mindset, making up your mind to learn and walk your talk, you become a new person and achieve more than you otherwise would have. Achieving a bigger goal and becoming a better you go hand in hand.

The steps to financial freedom are intertwined: as you make one step you position yourself to take the next. This is illustrated in getting out of debt and spending below your income. The very act of repaying your debt involves cutting back on some expenses and using the money thus saved to pay down your debt. Something had to give way. If you spend all you earn, nothing will be left to meet your debt obligations.

Hence in the process of getting out of debt, you get to spend below your income—a fundamental principle of financial freedom. You cannot break this law and become financially free no matter the size of your paycheck. If you spend all you earn, you become broke; if you spend more than you earn, you end up in debt. It's as simple as that no matter who you are.

By the time your debts are all paid off, you can channel the monthly debt payments into your savings and investments, rather than allow it to drip back into the spending pool where it will disappear without trace.

From insurance industry statistics, out of 100 people who start work at age twenty-two, by retirement age (sixty to sixty-five), one will be rich, four will be financially independent, fifteen will have some savings, and the remaining eighty will be either working, dependent on pensions, broke, or dead.

YOU CAN EARN BIG AND STILL GO BROKE

Some celebrities have violated this principle of spending below your income and paid dearly for it. There's a sad story of a man who lost his job at a car wash and ended up suing his employers for racial discrimination. He was fired for scratching customers' cars with his ring while waxing. His boss had warned him repeatedly about the ring to no avail. As customers' complains continued, the man was finally let go.

You may be wondering what was so special about the ring. Well, this guy was an ex-NFL star who'd taken the job at the car wash when he'd gone broke. He had won the ring as the most valuable player at the height of his professional career. It was all he had left of the millions of dollars he had earned. It was his most precious possession and asking him to remove it was the ultimate humiliation to him.

Stories abound of celebrities who became destitute after having hundreds of millions of dollars pass through their hands. Many professional boxers have come out of retirement due to cash flow problems. The millions they made in their heydays were gone with the wind. The same story plays itself out in the corporate world, where executives retire to poverty, with nothing to show for their former jet-set lifestyles.

To avoid this, you have to acquire the mind-set of spending below your income. If you don't have cash to cover a purchase, you cannot afford it; delay your gratification and wait until you do. Do not borrow to pay for things when you're short of cash, not even for the deposit for your home mortgage loan.

Spending *within* your income will not cut it. That's flirting with Brokeville. You need to save ten percent of your gross salary just as a starting point. As you progress on the journey, you'll become more creative and investment savvy and move to twenty percent, fifty percent, and, ultimately, one hundred percent.

Don't scream just yet. Getting there means developing multiple streams of income so you no longer need your salary to meet your monthly expenses. To achieve this, you will invest some of your savings for cash flow. If you're not ready to start investing, rather than park all your savings in a bank you can place it in higher-interest yielding money market instruments like term deposits, treasury bills, or bonds.

Just remember you will not get there overnight. Taking the first step is what's important.

THE 10-10-10-70 RULE

A good starting point is the 10-10-10-70 formula. I call it the
Jim formula since I first heard it from Jim Rohn.

The first ten percent is your tithes or gifts to a charity of your choice. The second ten percent is for saving and
investment by you (in a business, real estate, etc). The third
ten percent is savings for investing through others (stocks,
mutual funds, venture capital, etc). The seventy percent
that's left is what you live on. As your income increases,
you can gradually increase your savings rate and reduce your
expenditure.

For some living on seventy percent of their income might
be a real stretch. Trying to fit this into your current budget
might be mission impossible. There are two approaches:

- Slash your budget and make it fit. This needs a high level
  of courage and motivation that not everyone can muster.
  If you're married, your spouse may not be as eager as you
  are. There will be things you may be ready to give up but
  he or she will dig his or her heels in. Do what you can
  without rocking the boat.
- You can start with 1-1-1-97. This is doable for most as a
  start. You can then graduate to 2-2-2-94 and build up until
  you cross the 10-10-10-70 line on your way to wealth and
  abundance. By the way, the first three numbers do not all
  have to be the same.

As you keep going, the numbers will change. They will fall
in line with your goals, values, and level of personal growth
and development.

The fundamental principle of building and accumulating
wealth is to save and invest. If you spend below your income

and save every month, this becomes the seed money for your investment, which further accelerates your wealth-building process. If you spend within your income, spending all you earn month after month, your savings grows by zero percent and you remain in one inglorious spot. If you spend more than you earn, you're moving in the opposite direction, becoming poorer each month as you dig yourself deeper in debt and ultimately move toward bankruptcy.

You worked long and hard for your money. You should make it work hard for you so you can achieve financial freedom rather than give it away routinely month after month. If you keep giving all your money away, there will be nothing left for you, leaving you perpetually strapped to your job without options. If you get downsized, you'll find yourself in dire financial straits.

YOUR MONEY REFLEX

When you get into a car, your reflex is to reach for the seatbelt. If you touch a hot object, your reflex is to remove your hand. If a flying object comes at you, your reflex is to duck.

What is your reflex when it comes to money? What do you do instinctively the moment money comes to you?

For most, is the reflex is to spend. We give away money to get things rather than give things away to get money. The root of the problem is a lack of self-discipline and the inability to delay gratification in the short term.

This is a conditioned behavior from early childhood. Whenever we received money, our immediate impulse was to spend it. We loved sweet things—ice cream, candy—and money brought them to us, hence spending made us happy. Each time we went out with our parents, we asked them to buy stuff for us. Our parents capitalized on that as leverage to make us behave well. Hence good behavior amounted to our parents giving us money to buy things or buying things for us.

This conditioned response got carried over into adulthood. Now, anytime we received money, we want to get into that happy, feel-good state by spending—also known as *retail therapy*. We tend to treat money as hot coals that burn holes through our pockets, and we have to let go of it as soon as possible to avoid getting hurt.

Spending has become a pleasurable event while saving has become a painful exercise instead of the other way around. Have you seen the looks on people's faces as they come out of shops, lugging bags bulging with merchandise—often paid for by credit cards—that will soon end up in the trash?

Seeing your money disappear should be the hard part while seeing your money stay and grow should be the fun part. Instead our psychology is the reverse. Spending makes us feel so good. Little wonder we cannot hold on to money; rather, we repel it. For many, payday is a sad day because it's a stark reminder their salary is just not enough. But it wasn't enough five or ten years ago, and I can guarantee you it won't be enough in five or ten years' time either. *Enough* is a goalpost on wheels, moving away as your income inches closer. Your expenditures grow to catch up with your income. It's like chasing a mirage.

DO YOU REALLY NEED ALL THAT STUFF?

What you need to do, right here and right now, is pull over. Stop and really think. Ask yourself some hard questions, keeping in mind that folks who struck it rich started with virtually nothing compared to what has passed through your hands.

What happened to your income in the last five to ten years? Where did your money go?

What did you spend it on?

Where is the stuff you spent your money on?

What are you still spending your money on now?

Do you need to buy that new TV simply because it has the latest technology when your existing one has not packed up yet?

Do you need to have a TV for every room in your house as if you are running a hotel?

Do you need to pay for premium cable TV when you only watch a couple of stations a couple of times?

Do you need to buy the latest mobile phone while your existing phone is working fine?

What are you doing with more than one mobile phone?

Why trade in your car for a newer model when you haven't finished paying off your original loan?

Have you considered holding on to your car for two years or more and using the money you would spend to upgrade it on acquiring assets?

Can you fit your lifestyle in one car rather than struggle to maintain two or three?

Can you afford the private school your children are attending?

Have you considered the option of moving them to a cheaper private or public school and supervising their home work?

Can you really afford your home or apartment?

Have you considered the option of moving to a smaller place to ease your cash flow?

Can you save money by teaming up with friends and exercising in the neighborhood rather than paying for a gym membership you hardly use?

Rather than going on that exotic holiday, why not vacation locally and invest the money you would have spent in assets

Practical Steps to Financial
Freedom and **Independence**

that will generate sufficient cash flow in the future to pay for other exotic holidays?

Can you plan your trips in advance and take advantage of lowest fares? Why pay premium fares?

Before you write that check, is that item an asset or liability?

What will it be worth in five years?

Will it generate cash flow or go out with the trash?

If you must buy this item, is this the best time?

Why not wait until it goes on sale?

Have you evaluated the impact of this purchase on your financial goals? Will you regret this decision in five years?

Why do we spend money the way we do?

Why do we go for the expensive item when a cheaper one can do the job?

It takes courage to ignore what people will think or say when making spending decisions. It's natural to want to look rich, especially if our colleagues at work look affluent. We don't want to risk looking like the poor cousin. We want to show that we belong too. Thomas Stanley in *The Millionaire Mind* calls it *image affluence*.

MY STORY

Prior to commencing my journey to financial freedom, peer pressure was a major determinant in how I spent my money. I tried to stay within my income for monthly living expenses but borrowed when it came to items the public could see. I borrowed for the rental deposits on my first apartment, my wedding, and my first car. Anytime I needed to buy a big-ticket item and didn't have enough cash, I borrowed. I was working for an oil company and I felt I had to meet the standards expected of me.

As the foolishness of my actions dawned on me, I started to save and invest. I took my eyes off my affluent-looking colleagues and focused on rebuilding my financial foundation. Spending so much time on my computer and minding my business helped a great deal. I started to drop out of the social circuit and the pressures that went with it. Since I was hardly spending time with the Joneses, the pressure to catch up with them diminished. My focus became my asset portfolio. As my salary went up, my expenditure remained fixed while my savings and investment went up.

I currently live on thirty percent of my income. Seventy percent goes to giving, savings, and investment. I started out with Jim's formula and gradually progressed across the fifty-percent line. One of the key reasons my expenses are very low is some of them are legitimate business expenses as the chairman of my companies, from phone bills to automobile costs.

As my cash flow increases, that figure will gradually reduce from thirty percent to ten percent and below. This means the return from my investments grows while my expenditure remains fairly constant. There is only so much you can spend on food and clothing no matter how rich you become—unless you want to get in the news.

BANK YOUR INCREASE AND WINDFALL

What do you do when you get a salary increase or bonus at work? (Both the expected and surprise variety.) Most folks hear a rumble in the jungle. Needs and wants scream for attention; items hitherto not in the budget pound on the door, asking to be let in. More often than not, they get their way. A bonus goes toward a new car, a holiday overseas, home improvement, clothes, toys, you name it. Everything becomes a necessity all of a sudden and there is tumult and discontent until you capitulate.

Peace returns to the castle after all the money is all gone. You can see a palpable sense of relief in everyone's faces. The enemy has been repelled. You go back to status quo and calm returns. There has been no saving. If any of the enemy—cash—was missed in the offensive, it is fished out kicking and screaming and spent with glee. Life is good! Money is meant to be spent! Tomorrow will take care of itself.

But if you could live on your salary before the increase, why increase your expenditure when you get a raise?

Murphy's Law of expenditure states: expenses will always grow to meet income. If you operate under this law, your income will never be enough. Your expenditure will always catch up. More money will not make ends meet as the ends keep moving. More money will simply generate more expenses and more debts.

If you refuse to shift from the paradigm of *spending makes you happy* to the paradigm of *saving makes you happy*, simply make up your mind about what you need to live on, which should not depend on your income. This is where most people miss the plot. Your monthly living expense should be fixed, to be reviewed once in a blue moon if inflationary pressure warrants it (not pay-raise pressure). Everything else should go to savings, investment, tithes, and giving. It's not time to indulge yourself. Bank your increases, bonuses, and windfalls. Stick to your financial goals so the excess cash will not trickle back into the spending pool and disappear without a trace. If the raise is unexpected, that's all well and good; that means you'll get to exceed your financial goals for the year.

Leave no room for loose cash. Fix your expenses and if you come into some unexpected money, increase your savings to accelerate your attainment of your financial goals rather than your consumption.

IN SUMMARY

In order to save, you need to spend below your income. Allocate money for spending based on what's available after meeting your savings and financial goals rather than peer pressure and societal expectations. It's nice to please people, but wrecking your finances in the process is too high a price to pay.

- Determine upfront how much you need to live on based on your savings goals.
- Fix your expenses. Don't spend more when your income increases. Rather, save and invest more.
- Get started on the 10-10-10-70 rule. Save and invest before spending.
- Change your psychology and money reflex. Let saving make you happy rather than spending. Celebrate attainment of your financial goals.
- Stop accumulating stuff and get rid of excess stuff you have. Scale down your expenses, especially image-based ones.
- Invest your windfall—don't spend it.

7

PAY YOURSELF FIRST

A penny here, and a dollar there, placed at interest,
goes on accumulating, and in this way the desired
result is attained. It requires some training, perhaps, to
accomplish this economy, but when once used to it, you
will find there is more satisfaction in rational saving
than in irrational spending
—P.T. BARNUM

All the laws and principles of attaining financial freedom can be summarized as follows: pay yourself first.

The concept can be hard to grasp at first. It may be difficult to comprehend how changing the way you disburse your income can have a significant impact on your financial fortune. But it does. Paying yourself first is a paradigm shift, a reordering of priorities. It means putting saving above spending, enabling you save, invest, and develop multiple streams of income to fund the lifestyle you desire. It's about delayed gratification.

Paying yourself first is a shift from spending first and saving what's left to saving first and spending what's left. It takes the same amount of money but a different mind-set, and it has a different outcome. In short it's the surest way to spend below your income.

SAVE FIRST AND SPEND WHAT'S LEFT

Typically our focus is on spending. We pay our bills, house-keeping costs, and living expenses before we save what's left, if anything. More often than not, there's nothing left to save. This is called living from hand to mouth or from paycheck to paycheck.

When you pay yourself first, you save first and spend what's left. If the amount available for spending isn't enough to fund your current lifestyle, you'll be forced to scale down. If this doesn't cut it, the next step will be to find ways to increase your income rather than eliminate your savings.

Paying yourself first helps you to make your financial goal happen proactively rather than hoping and praying for it. However, it doesn't end with saving before spending. It also encompasses what you do with your savings. If you don't do something meaningful, the money gradually drips back into the spending pool and evaporates without a trace. You will have precious little to show for it except a mountain of stuff destined for the trash and a pile of debt.

To better understand paying yourself first, let's take a closer look at what it typically entails.

If you're like most people, you pay yourself last. You pay your bills, set money aside for housekeeping and living expenses, entertainment, and so on. You buy some impulse items not originally in your budget because subconsciously you regard any money in your salary account as available to spend. Then, if anything is left, you put it in your savings.

If a friend or family member needs a loan, you can't say you don't have the money since it's sitting there in your bank account. You know you may never see it again, but you don't want to be the bad guy. Against your better judgment, you empty your bank account.

YOUR NEW NET INCOME

Typically your salary is paid into your bank account. You only get to see your net income, or your gross income less taxes and deductions taken out at the payroll level—all the things you cannot see. You do not base your budget on your gross income because it's not available for spending. In your mind, you know it's not yours, although your employment letter clearly states it is.

If you're like most people, you equate your net income with your disposable income. This is where most people lose the plot. This means the amount that hits your account is available for spending after settling your bills. You have your recurrent monthly expenditure, and you have wants or wishes that feed on your monthly budget anytime there is available cash. That brilliant appliance you saw on TV, that cool gizmo you saw with a colleague at work, the latest phone, TV, game box, etc.—these items use up what's left of your money. They come before saving, which becomes a once-in-a-while affair if there are any leftovers. Usually there aren't.

Like your taxes, if you do not see your savings, you cannot spend it. If you have a holding account for your savings, do not allow it to tarry there. Make your money work hard for you in your business, stock portfolio, real estate, commodities trading, or whatever you prefer. Pay yourself first and spend below your income by deducting your planned savings (say ten percent minimum) from your gross income. You'll be left with less money to spend than usual and will have to make do with less.

For this to happen, you have to reduce your monthly expenditure. As illustration, let's assume you currently live from paycheck to paycheck. You want to pay yourself first in order to achieve your financial goal.

Let's assume as follows:

1. Monthly gross salary: $3,000,
2. Monthly taxes and deductions: $1,000.
3. Annual bonuses, allowances, etc. (net): $6,000
4. Monthly rent and utilities: $700
5. Monthly living expenses: $1,300

Your total net income is $2,000 per month x 12 ($24,000) plus $6,000, amounting to $30,000 per annum. This is what gets to your salary bank account.

SCENARIO 1: PAY YOURSELF LAST

You pay your bills and live on what's left—$1,300. You spend your bonuses and allowances on a foreign holiday, a new large-screen TV, the latest mobile phone and gizmos. You upgrade your car to the latest model. You satisfy your wants before saving, which means you hardly save.

SCENARIO 2: PAY YOURSELF FIRST

You have made the decision to be financially independent in five years. Your financial goal for the next twelve months is to save $12,000. You decide to save twenty percent of your gross monthly income, save $4,800 from your bonuses, and reduce your utility bills and living expenses. Your income and expenses look like this:

1. Monthly gross salary: $3,000
2. Net income (less taxes and deductions): $2,000
3. Annual bonuses, allowances, etc. (net): $6,000
4. Monthly savings (twenty percent of gross): $600
5. Annual savings from bonuses, allowances, etc.: $4,800
6. Monthly rent and utilities: $650
7. Monthly living expenses: $750

Total annual savings: $600 x 12 + $4,800 = $12,000

To make this happen, you deduct $600 from your net income and deposit it in an account to which you have no ready access. Rather than travel abroad, you vacation locally ($1,200). You hold on to your mobile phone, TV set, game console, etc. to ensure your savings target is met. You cut down on utilities and other luxuries and fit your lifestyle around $750 per month.

At first glance $750 may not seem sufficient for someone who has been living on $1,300. The first impulse will be to slash your savings and plough back into the spending pool. That's shooting yourself in the foot. If you're serious about your financial goal, and you're clear on what you need the $12,000 for, you'll find it easier to stand your ground and make it happen.

If you're very determined to break the vicious cycle, you can cut back on some unnecessary expenses, cut up your credit cards, reschedule some debts, and do without some so-called necessities for a season. You'll thereby use the pressure to fit in to your new, slimmer budget as motivation to eliminate wasteful spending and make do with less in the short term.

Necessity is the mother of invention. When you have to make do with less, you discover you can get a better deal by shopping somewhere else and there's not much difference between the brands you normally buy and cheaper brands. You can also work overtime in the interim to make your numbers work. You'll become a stronger and wealthier person in the process.

There are a thousand and one ways to lower your monthly expenses. There are thousands of personal finance websites and blogs that can teach you how. Where there's a will, there's a way. It may hurt in the beginning, but when you attain your financial goal it will be more than worth the effort.

MAKE YOUR MONEY WORK FOR YOU

We now get to the most important point—the main reason you're paying yourself first: to make your money work for you. You're not paying yourself first so you can admire how your $1,000 a month builds up over time, like Silas Marner. The $12,000 is to be invested in an income-generating asset. You can then choose to spend your profits or reinvest for bigger returns. This is the secret: to work hard to build assets to increase your cash flow.

The least you can do is to park the $1,000 a month in a money market instrument that yields at least eight percent per annum (you may need to save for a while to accumulate the minimum amount required). As you increase your balance by $1,000 every month, you increase the returns from a trickle to a flow. Based on your investment skills, you can invest the money for a twenty-five percent increase in the stock market, forex, real estate investment trusts (REIT), commodity and options trading, etc.

You have to find out what works best for you. If you forget everything else, don't ever forget the whole idea of paying yourself first is to build up your asset portfolio so as to generate additional cash flow streams—period. You can then use this additional cash flow to boost your standard of living while still sending $1,000 to work for you every month. You can also decide to reinvest your interest income for accelerated returns.

MY STORY

It took me a while to understand the concept of paying myself first. I initially could not figure out how changing the sequence of disbursing my income would make me richer. I was used to my salary not being enough, and I was forever praying for a raise and for the month's end to show up. I tried saving several times but I couldn't leave the money alone in the savings account. Rather than saving to keep, I was saving to spend. After several attempts, I gave up.

Then I read the book *Rich Dad, Poor Dad* by Robert Kiyosaki. In fact I read it three times before I got the hang of it. And what it taught me was this: focus on building assets to enable you pay for your liabilities (this is discussed in detail in Chapter 10). I had to send my money on an errand before my long, spending arms caught up with it.

A colleague at my office had introduced me to investing in the stock market way back in 1998. I bought some blue-chip stocks in a couple of transactions and promptly went back to my old ways. As my mind opened to the concept of paying myself first, I decided to put my investing in the stock market on autopilot, as that was the only investment outlet I was familiar with aside from money market accounts. I set up standing orders on my salary account for money to be transferred to the following accounts by direct debit:

• My children's school fees account
• My family emergency savings in a money market account
  I also issued twelve post-dated checks (one per month) to:

• My stockbroker
• My fund manager

My stockbroker took buy and sell orders from me while my fund manager had a free hand in managing my portfolio without my input. Having two stock portfolios enabled me to benchmark my performance with a professional fund manager. I also funded my insurance products as and when due before spending; that way my investments had precedence over spending.

My asset portfolio grew rapidly under the discipline of paying myself first. As the years went by, it became a habit. I moved from stocks to real estate just before the market went bust in 2007.

SHIFT YOUR FOCUS TO THE INCOME SIDE

The key benefit of paying yourself first, as stated earlier, is increasing your income through your investments. That means putting your savings to work for you. After fitting into your slimmer budget, the next step is to shift your focus immediately to the income side—to increasing your income. This shift makes all the difference.

The average person focuses on making ends meet. Don't fall into that trap. Focus on generating more income from your investments. As you keep your focus on the income side, you begin to discover more ways to generate multiple streams of income, increase your cash flow, and be able to afford what you really want. This is the main reason I chose the words "spend below your income" rather than "live below your means". Increase your means and live the life you really want rather than descend back to poverty mentality and living below your dreams. You cannot become very rich by saving alone. You have to increase your income by accumulating more assets.

Get the pressure to make ends meet work in your favor, not against you. Instead of murmuring, complaining, borrowing, and focusing mainly on how to get things cheaply or get cheap things, focus your energy on increasing your income. Excessive focus on making ends meet can make you cheap and develop a lack mentality, which becomes a self-fulfilling prophecy. When you focus on more income, it forces you to think out solutions and explore more investment options that increase your cash flow and increase your financial intelligence and acumen. You develop an abundance mentality and the belief you can afford anything so long as you can figure out how.

Focusing perpetually on how to make ends meet boxes you in to the arena of managing lack. Focusing on how to increase your income opens up limitless possibilities to make more and have what you really want. The key difference is where you place your focus. So, after making your budget work, move on. Don't settle. Start making your money work hard for you.

It bears repeating that if you pay yourself first and do not put the money to work hard for you immediately, it will end up in the spending pool and you will find yourself back at square one. If you still have some outstanding debt, paying yourself first can help you rapidly pay it off from the additional income stream—if you know what you're doing. Paying yourself first, if done correctly, can signal the turning point in your journey to financial freedom.

YOU DESERVE IT

Paying yourself first boosts your self-esteem. You honor yourself when you pay yourself first before spending. You send a strong message that:

> You are important.
> You are worthy of becoming wealthy.
> You deserve it.
> You can handle it.
> You can do it.
> You are not a slave to money.
> You are not working in vain.
> You have something to show for your work.

As your asset base grows each month, you are reinforcing the message that you are a man of integrity (oneness), that you are doing what you said you would do, and that you are moving a step closer to your financial goal and your dreams each month. You feel confident you are gaining control of your finances and your journey to financial freedom is doable. It's a good feeling that can inspire you to greater things.

IN SUMMARY

Paying yourself first is a shift of focus from spending to saving. Save first and spend what's left rather than spend first and save what's left, if anything. It's about a paradigm shift and reordering your priorities. This creates not passive savings but seed capital. That means you put your money to work hard for you to generate more income. If you save without putting the money to work, you will be tempted to dip your hands into it.

- Like taxes, deduct your savings before you pay your bills and monthly expenses.
- Spend within your new net income or disposable income. Keep your savings out of reach.
- Invest your savings to generate more income. You can use part of this new income to supplement your living expenses.
- Focus on making your money work harder for you rather than on making ends meet. Create abundance rather than become an expert in managing lack.
- Honor yourself by paying yourself first before spending.

8

AVOID BUDGET-BUSTING MONSTERS

A budget tells us what we can't afford, but it doesn't keep us from buying it.

——WILLIAM FEATHER

Spending above one's budget is a constant struggle for most. An increasing number of things attract our attention, transforming themselves from wants to needs fueled by advertising, who we hang out with, and what the Joneses are up to, while our ability to afford them remains limited by one source of income. Sticking to a budget looks like a losing battle. To avoid this feeling of constant defeat, we often abandon our budgets, bury our heads in the sand, and take things as they come. We spend on what we believe are the bare necessities and keep spending until we run out, and then credit comes to the rescue.

Ignoring our challenges will not make them go away. If you ignore a beggar, he will go away after a while. If you ignore your budget, you make your financial situation progressively worse and out of control. Your budget is a key tool for controlling your finances. You have to find a way to make it work.

Your first port of call is your mind-set. You have to change it from always giving all your money away to keeping some by paying yourself first. That means you have to value money over things. Rather than raid your bank account to go buy things, raid your things to go change them to cash. Rather than cash to trash, switch from trash to cash. Stop accumulating things and start accumulating wealth. Rather than building up liabilities (things that don't generate cash flow), build up assets. In summary, rather than repelling cash, attract cash.

The next step is to limit your access to it. By paying yourself first, as discussed in detail in the previous chapter, and keeping the money and credit cards out of your reach, you have burnt your bridges and have no choice but to live with what you have. Leave yourself no fallback position. You have no choice but to stick to your budget. If you make mistakes like robbing Peter to pay Paul, you pay for it, and the pain of sorting out Peter will make you stay on the straight and narrow way tomorrow.

No matter your good intentions, there are things that can easily trip you up on the way to sound budgetary discipline. I call them *budget-busting monsters*. They come against your budget from all directions, making sure things don't add up, that you end up in the red month after month. The insidious thing about these monsters is that most of them are inside jobs. They sabotage us from within. You cannot run away—you always take them with you.

One thing common to all of them is that you can avoid them, and you can weaken their power over you and the damage they do to your budgets and finances.

Here they come:

THE IMPULSE MONSTER

This one is an inside job triggered mostly by sight. This monster comes alive when we see something we really like, something that would really be nice to have but is not in our budget. It follows us as we go down the store aisles, seeing stuff we believe will make us happier and our lives better. We did not plan to buy these things when we left home but they somehow end up in our shopping basket and follow us to the checkout.

This monster does not give up, even when it loses the battle of the aisle. It lays an ambush at the checkout. With the active connivance of the store, a rack is set up right next to the checkout, filled with impulse items. They stare at us as we unpack our baskets for the cashier to scan. Prodded by this monster, some of the impulse items join the pile, sneaking in before the cashier asks with that bewitching smile, "Is that all?"

Then a hush descends as we await the total from our exploits. We stifle a gasp when the total flashes on the screen. It's too late to back out now. There's a crowd of impatient shoppers behind you waiting to check out. All eyes are on you. The teller is waiting for payment.

Cursing yourself inwardly for doing it again, you surrender your plastic to further deplete your savings. You obviously don't have enough cash to cover the impulse, hence your card comes to the rescue. You are torn between the euphoria of your new purchases and the new dent on your bank account. With mixed feelings you roll your trolley out of the store, wondering if you have enough money left for the other items you actually planned to buy.

Sometimes, if the damage is not much, you throw in more impulse items after your totals have been tallied and pay for them separately.

How do you contain this monster from its frequent rampaging runs? Stick to your budget and ignore the monster's antics. Make a list before you go out the door and shop strictly by it. Pay only cash for your purchases so you're not tempted to flash your plastic. When you run out of cash, it's time to head back home—period. If there are many things left to be bought, it serves you right. Next time you'll stick to your list. This will force you to prioritize and buy first things first. It may take a while to get a handle on this, but stick with it long enough and your numbers will start to add up.

MY STORY

I remember when my wife was pregnant with our first son, Josh. She had a craving for guava fruit and sent me one late evening to the grocery store to pick a couple for her. Off I went to Tesco, a five-minute walk from where we lived.

As I made my way to the fruits section, I remembered we were low on bananas. As two bunches landed in my shopping basket, the show began. I reached for apples, oranges, tangerines, cucumbers, pears, and finally guavas. I was not done yet. It would be nice to get some biscuits and other stuff to nibble. Pregnant women love nibbling. I wheeled around.

This was in the days before mobile phones were common and my wife was worried sick over what must have become of me. She barely restrained herself from dialing 911. I came home an hour later, laden with four heavy grocery bags. So much for a couple of guava fruits!

I have since discovered the ingenious invention called the shopping list. Now I shop like a guided missile. I look at my list, home in on the right aisle, grab what I need, and head for the checkout.

THE IMAGE MONSTER

This monster is forever persuading you to step up and match your image or status in society. It tells you your car doesn't fit your status, and your dress and jewelry don't fit your image. You need to upgrade. You need a car and a house to match your neighborhood, and furniture to match the house. Then you need clothes and fashion accessories to match your car, a school for your children to match your image, and the list goes on and on. Functionality is no longer an issue, just the image the items portray.

You buy top of the range designer brands—even in bottled water, orange juice, perfumes, everything. It all has to match. Image is everything, this monster tells you again and again. There is no second opportunity to make a good first impression. So you spend yourself deeper and deeper into a hole to make a good impression.

This monster is green-eyed with envy and covetousness, and almost crossed-eyed from looking at what's happening over the fence so you can play catch up. If the Joneses buy the latest model SUV, yours is due for a trade-in. If John buys a new laptop, yours suddenly becomes too slow. If Mark buys the latest wide-screen TV, the picture quality of yours suddenly seem dull. If a new technology comes to town (3-D and co.), yours has just outlived its usefulness.

When we box ourselves into this corner, always maintaining our image and playing catch-up, we are forever buying the same thing over and over again. We change everything the moment a new model hits the shops, racking up debt or wiping out our savings to stay in the game. We easily lose sight of the fact that we are fixed to one inglorious spot, rapidly burning cash without any progress in savings, investing, and wealth accumulation. We get so caught up with being in step with the Joneses we lose sight of the fact that we have lost our way.

You need to STOP and check in to a spending rehab. Your mind is playing games with you, making you buy things you don't need with money you don't have to maintain an image that won't last. You need a new mind-set to deal with this monster. Spending is an emotional decision, and the moment you convince yourself you need something and you have access to cash, you are a goner. You have to kick your addiction to liabilities and acquire an asset addiction. This addiction makes you richer and, ultimately, able to afford your beloved luxuries.

THE SALES! SALES! MONSTER

This monster is relentless and merciless. It sells you the lie that you can save by spending. "Fifty percent off!" it screams. "Buy one, get one free! Get it for half price, despite the fact that this item does not feature in your current budget! "Buy now, think later!"

It bombards your budget when you're most vulnerable— Christmas, New Year's, Easter, Thanksgiving, Mother's Day, it hardly lets up. It watches out for a season of goodwill, when folks give in to the high street-induced atmosphere and let down their guard. Then it strikes. The deal looks very lucrative. You will never get it at this price.

How many items have you bought on sale that you never got around to using?

Sticking to your budget keeps this monster at bay. When you have just enough to meet your budget, you have no choice but to stick to it. If you spend on items not in your budget, then you only have yourself to blame. Plan your purchases ahead of time and instead of this monster depleting your bank balance, you can ride on its back and really make good savings.

THE ADVERTISING MONSTER

This monster is very deadly though it only barks, not bites. It doesn't attack your budget directly. It goes for your mind and emotions, where the action is.

The advertising monster bombards you from all directions. There's no hiding place, not even in the loo. It wears down your defenses, takes over your subconscious, and works on you gradually, and before you know it you're sold. It waits for the kill in the store aisle, when the item looms into view. You find yourself reaching out for it. You will bear the consequences later, but you just have to have it now. It often works in concert with the impulse monster, joining forces with other monsters to run a ring round you. Surrounded and outnumbered, you give in.

This monster comes at you at every waking moment. In magazines and newspapers, on TV and radio, on the road, it dominates the landscape with giant billboards and neon signs. You enter the train station and it's everywhere, on free newspapers, inside the wagon, and on the tunnel walls. There is no hiding place. You step out and it's on the buses and taxis. Sometimes, if you're not careful, you can hear its soundtrack playing in your head. You're simply surrounded.

This monster does not attack frontally. It's very gentle and patient. It uses repetition to wear down your defenses. It makes subtle suggestions over and over again until you believe them: Your car is too old and lacks the latest features and technology. Your home entertainment system is obsolete. Your computer is too slow. Your fashion is out of date. Your house is too small. Your life is too dull. It goes on and on. This monster normally leads the attack, then steps back and allows the others to finish the job.

The best way to contain this monster is to have a firm mindset and define who you are and where you're going (financial goals, etc.), and refuse to be intimidated. Have a plan and stick to it. This monster is deadly if you have loose cash hanging around your pocket or savings or on an unused credit card. Without available cash, this monster is powerless. It will shout itself hoarse and fizzle out.

You always have to be on your guard against this monster. It never ever gives up and never will. If you're resolute, you can tune it out completely until you're good and ready to entertain it—when you're actually in the market for the item it wants you to buy.

THE EASY CREDIT MONSTER

This monster works in concert with the last four monsters. The previous four soften you up, getting you in the ready-to-spend mood while the fifth goes for the jugular, making that purchase possible. You have run out of money, but you really must buy this. It's too good a deal to pass up. Offer expires tonight. Tomorrow you buy full price. This is your last opportunity.

Then the fourth monster appears on the scene. "You can have it," it says. "Zero down payment. Free credit. Take it home, start paying next year." Bingo! You're back in business. Shopping continues.

When you get home, more credit cards arrive in the mail—all preapproved. Zero-percent balance transfers, zero-percent interest for one year. The party goes on. It does not show you the mammoth two-percent-a-month, twenty-eight percent APR interest. This is hidden in the small print. Spend now, think later...

You can put this monster out of business simply by spending below your income and spending cash only or a debit card linked to your spending account. Make it a matter of policy not to use an ATM card on your savings account. Decline it, or cut it up when it arrives. Your savings account should be a one-way street—deposits only except in emergencies. Stick to your disposable income (available to spend after taxes, savings, and deductions). If you must make a purchase using your credit card, set up a direct debit to your spending account to clear the balance at each payment cycle, effectively operating on zero-percent APR. This way you're using your credit card as a debit card and enjoying the benefits of a credit card on zero-percent APR.

THE INFLATION MONSTER

This monster barges in uninvited. You have no control over it. It eats away your disposable income gradually and aggravates your already fragile financial position. Like the weather, this monster cannot be avoided; you can only prepare against it through sound personal financial management.

The first impulse is to throw more money into the spending pool. Avoid this if you can, though that's easier said than done if you're married. Embarking on this journey with your spouse will make decision making much easier and rancor-free.

If you take a good look at your budget, you may find where you're over-spending, not getting maximum value for your money, etc. It may mean shopping somewhere else. It may mean ignoring the image monster and buying a cheaper but equally good alternative. It may also mean doing without some nice things that are not necessary. There may be things you're paying for that you can do without, or you can find cheaper or free alternatives (e.g. cable TV). You may find out while tackling this monster that you actually can reduce your monthly expenses.

THE EMERGENCY MONSTER

This is another monster that comes uninvited. It breaks down the front door, bringing with it unexpected events both human and mechanical: medical emergencies, major car repairs, natural disasters, taking in a stranded relative, etc. The death of a loved one is this monster at its meanest.

The emergency monster can be contained by preparing for it before it shows up. You can do this by having insurance and a savings account for emergencies and keeping it out of reach on a day-to-day basis. You and your spouse will have to decide upfront what constitutes an emergency, and the amount you'll keep in the account will depend on your circumstances.

THE LAYOFF MONSTER

Like its cousin the emergency monster, this one breaks down the front door—and then carries it away in its wake. The clouds may gather, but you may have no inkling this monster is heading for you. One day you have a job, the next you're out in the cold. This is the deadliest of all the monsters. It doesn't just bust your budget; it sends it into a fatal tailspin.

The surest antidote against the sting of this monster is multiple streams of income. Every home should aim for at least three or four. Depending on one source of income is flirting with financial disaster. Job security went out with the Industrial Age. With globalization and the Information Age, jobs are now without borders. An event or trend on one end of the globe can make you out of work tomorrow even if you didn't catch the headline news.

You need to be in a position where if your salary or earned income goes, life goes on without a blink. If your salary constitutes up to seventy-five percent of your income, you're naked to the onslaught of this monster. By the time it's done with you, you'll be like a hurricane victim.

Another antidote against this monster is to maintain the equivalent of six months of your take-home pay in a special, out-of-bounds savings account. Some recommend six months of living expenses. I prefer take-home pay as life has to go on after a job loss. You still have school fees to pay, medical bills, you name it.

Again, this savings account has its limitations. The assumption is that within six months you will land another job. This is not always the case, especially in a global economic crisis. Also, as you cross the fourth month, panic may start to set in. You start pondering "what if" as the sixth month approaches.

With multiple streams of income, you can sleep easily, knowing this monster usually strikes one income source at a time. In the unlikely event that two income sources are knocked out in one fell swoop, you still have something to hold on to as you rebuild the damaged income streams or develop new ones.

IN SUMMARY

Staying within your budget can be a constant struggle for some. In order to work successfully with your budget, you need to avoid budget busters.

- Impulse: Stick to your list and carry just enough cash to cover your list. Cut down on window shopping.
- Image: Be real. Cut your coat according to your cloth rather than public perception of your size. If high rent,

mortgage, or school fees are threatening to drown you financially, swallow your pride and scale down accordingly.

- Sales: Only buy things on your list when they are on sale. There's no way you can save money by spending. No matter how much the price is reduced, you end up with less money.

- Advertising: Nobody can make you do what you don't want to do. Make up your mind to stick to your list and focus on your financial goals and you will do just fine.

- Easy credit: Only buy stuff you can pay cash for. If you don't have enough cash, wait until you do. Do not take up new consumer debt. Pay off existing loans.

- Inflation: Find a way to make your budget work rather than reduce your savings. Do comparison shopping. You may find better deals elsewhere.

- Emergency: Prepare for emergencies before they happen. Have insurance and a savings account for worst-case scenarios.

- Layoff: Have a plan in case you're laid off from your job. Develop multiple streams of income. Keep a reserve of three to six months of take-home pay in the event you find yourself out of work.

9

INVEST IN YOUR FINANCIAL EDUCATION

Have you built your castles in the air? Good, that is where it should be built. Now go to work and build foundations under them.

—HENRY DAVID THOREAU

After saving by paying yourself first, you need to have your money work hard for you. Parking it in the bank to earn little or no interest is like leaving your money in idle mode. With an interest rate much lower than the inflation rate, your money will be worth less and less the longer it stays in the bank.

You need to invest your money to accelerate its growth and rate of return as you progress in your journey to financial freedom. Before you begin investing, you need to invest first in your financial education—in becoming your own financial expert.

When it comes to investing, most people turn over their money to experts—strangers, really—hoping they know what they're doing and will deliver a superior return on investment as promised in their brochures. There's nothing wrong with consulting an expert. As a matter of fact, you need to go through a broker to trade in the stock market and other markets.

What is wrong is:

Not knowing what you're doing.
Not having a clue whether the advice you're given is right or not.
Not being able to differentiate between a sales pitch and financial advice.
Not knowing the right questions to ask in order to get the right answers.
Not knowing how to tell a good broker from a mediocre one.
Swallowing everything you're told hook, line, and sinker.

BECOME YOUR FINANCIAL EXPERT

When it comes to investing, you have to be in the driver's seat rather than handing over the wheel and hoping someone else will take you to your desired destination safely. The main disadvantage of relying on a broker or financial adviser to make your investment decisions is that most brokers are broke (no disrespect intended). They are employees who depend on salaries that come from commissions. The more you buy and sell, the more money they make.

Brokers hardly put their money where their mouths are. Most do not take their own advice. They offer you a shirt while they're topless. They advise you to invest in a stock they haven't invested their own money in, and when it all goes wrong you take the hit. Don't misunderstand me—brokers and financial advisers are good people. They're under constant pressure to make the right decisions, as they take the flack when things go wrong and may lose their jobs if they leave behind a trail of dissatisfied clients.

> *Wall Street is the only place that people ride to*
> *in a Rolls Royce to get advice from those that ride the*
> *subway.*
> —WARREN BUFFET

The key issue is being in control. You know your desired destination more than anyone else and have the most to lose if you don't make it there. Others can only offer their sincere sympathy or condolences.

The first step is to invest in your financial education. Become your own financial expert. Don't go in cold. Investing is not rocket science if you know what you're doing. The big problem is that most people have no clue what they're doing. They ride the wave of market sentiments, buy high, and sell low. If you want to perform surgery, you first of all go to medical school. If you want to drive, you go to a driving school. If you want to invest, you learn how to invest before you commit your hard-earned money to a game where you do not know the rules.

People have varied reasons for jumping right into an investment without a clue what's really going on.

- Some are penny wise and pound foolish. They think investment seminars are too expensive. They believe it's cheaper to do it yourself, to learn on the job. They save hundreds and lose tens of thousands.

- Some feel they have no time to commit to learning how to invest in the market they're interested in. They feel the shortcut is to consult an expert. They have time for TV, social outings, and working overtime but not to learn how to make their money work hard for them.
- Some feel it's too much trouble. After finishing college and earning a degree, learning a new subject is too much stress. It's better to stick to what they know best.
- For others the world of finance looks like Latin—only a few can understand it. They feel since they do not have accounting degrees, they will not be able to wrap their brains around the subject of investing. Nothing could be further from the truth. Investing has its own language which any one can learn. A slab of numbers in company results or finance pages of newspapers tell a story. Only those who understand the language can understand what it's saying. The financially illiterate go straight to the bottom line— profit or loss, P/E ratios, or revenue projections.

Nothing enduring comes easy. There are tons of books and seminars and websites on investing. There's investing for dummies, investing for fools, www.foools.co.uk. If fools and dummies can learn to invest, then I'm afraid you've just run out of excuses.

The issue of time has to do with priority and where you want to end up in life. It's your choice to make. If you want to spend your life working hard for money rather than having your money work hard for you, it's your call.

INVESTMENT IS NOT RISKY—FINANCIAL ILLITERACY IS

Financial literacy is critical in your journey to financial freedom. If you decide to settle in a foreign country, you'd better learn the language. You can hope you'll always run across someone with a smattering knowledge of English to bail you out, but that's just getting by. If you want to flourish and succeed, you have to learn the language.

Financial literacy helps you analyze investments and make sound decisions that will bring superior returns on your money. Experienced investors can earn 25 to 10,000 percent returns on their investment. They know how to evaluate risks and understand the interplay between risk and reward. All it takes is knowledge and experience. The key is to know what you're doing. When you don't know what you're doing, you're gambling with your money. Investing is not risky. The investor is—an investor who doesn't know what he's doing.

You need bring on brokers and investment advisers as you venture into the world of investing. You have to know how to recruit the best hands for your team. You cannot take on a broker simply because your colleague in the office is using him. You need a broker who will give you advice tailored to your financial goals rather than treat you like a statistic. Someone who has been there, done that, and is willing to show you the way.

The quality of advice you get depends on the quality of questions you ask, which depends on the depth of your knowledge about investing. Investment education will help you in the following ways when dealing with a broker or financial adviser:

- You'll be in a better position to interview and select the right broker or adviser for your team. You'll know the right questions to ask. You'll be able to tell if the adviser knows what he's talking about. He'll work for you and should not be brought onto your team unless you've done proper due diligence including recommendations from folks you respect who are ahead of you in the journey.

- You can tell if the advice is good for you. You're not bound to swallow whatever you're told. The quality of answers you get is based on the quality of questions you ask. If you ask the right questions, you get the right answers. There are things you will not be told unless you ask. A good question to ask is how the broker's portfolio is doing and what he invests in.

- You'll access better investments. They come wholesale and retail. Experienced and knowledgeable investors are given access to wholesale investments (e.g. private placements) while the masses can only access retail (publicly traded stocks). Your broker will offer you investment options based on your knowledge and sophistication.

Investment education increases your risk tolerance and gives you access to much higher returns on your investment, which average investors have no access to. In regulated markets high-yield investments are reserved for people who understand the game and comply with SEC rules to access those types of investments. Margin loans are extended to accredited investors, not every Tom, Dick, and Harry. In the Nigerian stock market crash of 2008, thousands of rookie investors ended up with a pile of margin loan debts that they should not have had access to in the first place.

The leverage of other people's money is a two-edged sword. It can increase your returns exponentially or leave you with a mountain of debt. When the price of a stock with which you secured margin loans to purchase crashes and the lender calls in the loan, your loss is magnified. You're forced to sell the stock at a low price and end up with a capital shortfall coupled with escalating interest charges. If you used your own funds for the transaction, you would have had the option either to hold your position for the prices to recover or to cut your losses and sell. With a margin loan, you do not have that control. An experienced investor knows that control is the name of the game.

High-yield investments appear high risk to the average investor, but to the experienced investor who knows what he's doing it's an excellent opportunity. Your depth of investment knowledge determines your return on investment. The masses play on the fringes and get slaughtered when markets slump.

At each market crash a transfer of wealth occurs. As others cry, some are clinking glasses in celebration. A sophisticated investor makes money in bullish and bearish markets. Heads or tails, they win. Common people who have no clue what's going on except what their brokers tell them are left to pick up the pieces. The experienced investor has entry and exit strategies and is the first to exit before a crash. The rookie investor is left stranded on the beach at low tide.

SCHOOL SMARTS AND STREET SMARTS

To graduate from the investments of the poor and middle class (two percent to twenty-five percent annual return) to the investments of the rich (ultra-high returns—twenty-five percent to infinity), you need to invest in your financial education. A college degree gives you a job, but financial education gives you a life. Academic education makes you school smart while financial education makes you street smart and without that you will not flourish in the world. You may earn a fat salary but struggle financially.

Financial literacy is a major key to financial freedom. If you lack it, you're in for a lifetime of financial struggle. If you don't know how money works, you'll work for those who do. He who has the gold makes the rules. You can have a PhD and end up working for a college dropout.

The Forbes list is not a roll call of academic giants but folks with good business and financial acumen. With financial literacy, you have the tools to regain control of your finances, invest for exponential returns, exit the rat race and live your dreams.

MORE MONEY IS NOT THE ANSWER

Most people think more money will solve their financial problems. It actually magnifies an existing problem of financial illiteracy. If you have a badly leaking bucket, pouring in more water will not make it stay full. You have to plug the leak first.

Have you ever wondered why the salary increases, bonuses, and promotions you have gotten over the years have not solved your financial problems? The reason you are perpetually broke is financial illiteracy. When you are literate, you don't need someone else to tell you what to do, what to invest your money in, or which stocks to buy. They can only advise you. With financial education you have what it takes to navigate your way through the maze to your desired destination. It's the best investment you will ever make.

MY STORY

My financial education commenced in 2001, when I first read *Rich Dad, Poor Dad* by Robert Kiyosaki. I realized how little I know about personal finance and investing. My desire to learn was reawakened, and I went on to read other books in the Rich Dad series—*Cash Flow Quadrant*, *Rich Dad's Guide to Investing*, and *Retire Young, Retire Rich*. I went online, looking for material on personal finance and investing. I signed up for newsletters and subscribed to magazines like *Bloomberg*. I was eager to learn as much as I could.

I soon got a call from a broker. I allowed him to persuade me to buy shares of Luxury Brands Group, an upcoming fashion luxury brand listed in the UK second-tier stock market AIM with plans to get listed in the London Stock Exchange. I was excited to finally be in action. I was reassured the share price of 44p was very good to own a piece of a company that made dresses for the Queen of England and was concluding plans to bring on Prada. I eagerly mailed the check for 1,300 pounds sterling and waited for the company to make the news and get listed on the London Stock Exchange.

I also got calls from the US from a company trying to sell me oil futures. Although I was excited, I knew I did not know enough about options trading to take that plunge.

Upon return to Nigeria in 2003 and studying further, I realized the foolishness of my investing in a company I was introduced to on the phone without doing proper due diligence. Things fell apart. The deal with Prada fell through. The shares of Luxury Brands Group nosedived to 4p per share. I was shell-shocked. Mercifully, under new management, the company was reorganized and the shares bounced back to 21p per share. I was so relieved I didn't bother to wait for it to get back to my entry price of 44p. I cut my losses and ran for the exit.

I lost more than 600 pounds sterling, but I learned the hard lesson of not depending on a broker to make my investment decisions. I continued my financial education and started investing in the stock market in Nigeria. My search for financial education led me to the Moneywise Group, a company that teaches personal finance and investing through seminars, books, audio products, and publications including a weekly personal finance and investing newspaper, *Moneywise*. I bought shares in the company somewhere along the line and eventually became a member of the board.

IN SUMMARY

You would not want to drive a car without license or insurance. Apart from the fact that it's against the law, that would be foolish. You will wreck the car sooner or later. The same applies to investing without financial education. You're investing blind. You simply do not know what you're doing. You're only hoping the broker knows. That's a weak position to be in, especially when it involves your hard-earned money.

- Investing is not risky. Investing without financial literacy is.
- Without financial education, you don't have good entry and exit strategies. You enter at the wrong time and exit at the wrong time and take losses.
- Become your own financial expert. Do not invest blind, depending on others to make investment decisions for you—especially those who have something to gain from that transaction.
- Do not invest until you become an investor.

10

LET YOUR ASSETS BUY YOUR LUXURIES

Don't tell me where your priorities are. Show me where you spend your money and I'll tell you what they are.
—JAMES W. FRICK

Spending below your income does not amount to taking a vow of poverty. You can still indulge in a luxury or two while on your journey to financial freedom by acquiring assets to pay for your luxuries. Some are also necessities, e.g. a car, a vacation to unwind, living in a decent neighborhood, etc.

One thing you have to get crystal clear is that your salary is not your profit but your capital. If you mix this up, you're in for a lifetime of financial struggle.

If you think your capital is profit, you will spend it. Many employees lack capital to start their businesses because they spend it. You invest capital and take profits. The smart investor goes a step further by reinvesting his profits to get higher returns. This is delayed gratification in action.

You worked hard for your salary—it's a reward for your labor. But that does not make it your profit. Your income is your capital and your primary role is to convert it into assets. This is your key to sustainable financial breakthrough. Praying and fasting helps, but without assets you will have to labor before you earn. Your assets should pay for your luxuries (which are also liabilities) rather than your income.

The rate at which you convert income to assets determines your progress toward financial freedom and independence. Proceeds from your assets are what you spend on luxuries. If your income is not creating assets, you will be forced to fall back on your income to spend on luxuries. This means money leaves and nothing returns. It's no wonder you have precious little left from all your years of hard labor.

GONE WITH THE WIND

If you use your earned income to buy luxuries, when the item reaches the end of its useful life, your money and the item are gone for good. Typically you use your earned income to pay for your dream car, the latest game console, a widescreen 3-D HDTV, vacations, you name it. There is absolutely nothing wrong with enjoying the fine things of life. What is unwise is that years down the road, your money and what you spent it on will both be gone. You'll be left with nothing except check stubs and memories.

Let's take your car for example. You paid for it with your savings from salary or bonuses (your earned income). Six years down the road, your car is history and so is the money you spent on acquiring and maintaining it.

Now imagine you invested that money in a business, an investment property, or the stock market (or whatever you are comfortable with) instead and generated the cash flow required to buy your dream car.

You may have to wait a year, two years, or more. Your colleague at work who went ahead and bought that same car will look good while you look like the poor neighbor for a season. But by the time your asset generates enough cash flow to buy that car, you'll end up with:

1. The latest model of your dream car.
2. The business or asset you created.
3. The cash flow the asset is generating.

You now have an asset that can generate cash flow to replace the car when you eventually get tired of it. As for your colleague, all he has is his aging car. In four to six years his car will be due for replacement and he'll be figuring out financing options (savings, loans, etc.) for replacement. Two friends, same income, but different mind-sets; one is struggling financially while the other is getting richer by the day.

MY STORY

I paid dearly for my ignorance of this principle. I feel sad anytime I think of the money that passed through my hands in my early working years, never to return.

I worked for an engineering company for fifteen years. As a design engineer, I travelled abroad to many cities to work on different oil and gas projects. While on a tour of duty, my salary was paid into my bank account at home and I was paid a per diem to cover my hotel bills, transportation, etc.

Based on the duration of my assignment, I often travelled with my family. We lived below our means and saved a lot of money abroad, often by living in the cheapest part of town, using flat-share arrangements, travelling by bus rather than by train, and so on. I felt cool whenever we returned home awash with foreign currency and cash in the bank.

Sadly, six months later, all the money was always gone. Cars, the latest home appliances, and new wardrobes were all I had to show for my work. Years down the road, they too were all gone. All I had left was a photo album of memories. The word *asset* was not part of my vocabulary then.

With all the money gone, the next step was to pray for another tour of duty, and the cycle continued. More than ten years later, all I had left was a piece of land in a neighboring state that I had bought in a cheap settlement. I suffered from acute financial diarrhea. I could not hold on to money for long. I always gave it away. I was heading nowhere financially.

After I came to my senses, I started building assets. I invested consistently in the stock market, started a business, and invested in high-interest yielding money market instruments. A new world opened to me. Each car I have bought since then has been from the proceeds of my investments. The first car came from the sale of bonus shares in my stock portfolio. The second car was paid for by my business. I built my dream home in less than a year without having to break the bank. I still have a stock portfolio, and the business is growing bigger. Without these assets I would have had to wipe out my savings and borrow some too to make this all happen.

DELAYED GRATIFICATION

You can have it all by acquiring assets to pay for your lifestyle. All it takes is a bit of financial intelligence and delayed gratification. A minor adjustment in your mind-set can make a world of difference in your life.

Focus your energies on acquiring assets rather than liabilities and you will see your cash flow and net worth start to head in the right direction. Your salary income is not your profit but your capital. Your job is to convert it to assets that will generate the cash flow you desire.

As your cash flow increases, you will get to the point that you no longer need your salary to fund your monthly and annual expenses. When you get to this point, one hundred percent of your salary goes to investments. You now have the choice to continue working for love or kiss your bosses goodbye.

IN SUMMARY

The discipline of delayed gratification is required to save, invest, and use the proceeds of the investment to buy whatever luxury you desire rather than consume your income, which is your capital for investment. You can eat your cake and have it when you invest first and spend the proceeds rather than spend first and have nothing to invest.

- Convert your income into assets.
- Grow the assets to generate sufficient cash flow.
- Pay for your luxury without liquidating the assets.
- Continue growing the assets.

11

MIND YOUR BUSINESS

The best way to predict your future is to create it.
—PETER DRUCKER

Mind your business in the context of financial literacy simply means becoming the CEO of your life. For most people their employer determines where they live, how much they earn, what free time they have, and ultimately how far they can go in life. They go in young and vibrant and come out old and spent.

This is not advocating disloyalty to your employer or quitting your job. It's a call to take full responsibility for your personal development in your free time. Jim Rohn says you should put more energy into developing yourself than you put into your job. You become a better employee when you grow as a person, as you transition from being a follower to becoming a leader. Businesses need leaders to grow.

A typical employee spends most of his time minding other people's businesses. He spends his free time supporting his favorite team, watching his favorite TV programs, hanging out with his friends, attending every event he's invited to (and gate-crashing some)—anything but minding his own business.

There are four types of people on the planet:

1. Those who make things happen.
2. Those who carry the news of what's happening.
3. Those who watch things happening.
4. Those who don't know what's happening.

This can be further collapsed into two groups: actors and spectators.

WHAT'S YOUR BUSINESS?

Minding your business means belonging to the first group: those who make things happen, or actors. It means taking responsibility for your life and destiny. It means minding your business—literally.

Everybody is into business in one form or another, and it all involves selling. It's not enough to have a damn good product; you also have to be a damn good salesperson. That's one key reason why good writers do not necessarily become best-selling authors or the brightest employees do not become CEOs. How you package and sell your product is crucial.

An employee sells his service (time and skills) to earn income. He sells himself by preparing a resume or curriculum vitae and making good first impressions in interviews while looking for the highest bidder. Some employees go to new continents if the price is right. Upon getting the job, the selling continues as he packages himself as a strong contender for the vacancy upstairs. He climbs the corporate ladder.

You have to develop the skills required to take you where you desire to go. You have to own the process by minding your own business.

JOB DISSATISFACTION

Many employees are trapped in the wrong careers or wrong jobs. Most do not experience job satisfaction. A 2004 survey by *Businessweek* showed eighty-seven percent of Americans hate their jobs. A similar 2007 survey by Conference Board showed seventy-two percent of American executives believe they're not in their dream jobs.

With the global economic meltdown, the figures may be higher as more employees cling to jobs they hate out of fear of the unknown. A job is seen simply as a meal ticket and an income source. Degrees are acquired based on parental advice, dictated by trends in the marketplace, and governed by prestige in society. If the good jobs are in the oil and gas or telecoms sectors, the way to go is to obtain degrees that will get your foot in those doors. Dreams and passion become luxuries you'll indulge in after retirement, at age sixty or sixty-five.

Minding your business means finding your way back to where you belong. Doing what you love and loving what you do is a match made in heaven. It's a place where passion, talent, skills, aptitude, and purpose meet. You get paid while having fun. Work feels like play. Sadly very few find this place. A lot of people have good ideas about where it is but don't believe it's possible to get there. They believe doing what you love won't pay the bills, so they say goodbye to their dreams and hold on to the security that comes with a guaranteed salary.

By minding your business during your spare time, you can develop the skills and acumen to make your dream come true. You can make what you love doing profitable if you're willing to pay the price.

INVEST IN YOUR PERSONAL DEVELOPMENT

The best investments you can ever make are in yourself and in your personal growth and development. To be able to set and achieve goals, you need to know what to do and possess the self-discipline to follow through and remain focused, persistent, and hard-working until you achieve the desired results. Many know what to do. Few have the ability to follow through and accomplish it.

According to peak performance coach Anthony Robbins, success is eighty percent psychology and twenty percent mechanics. Having the ability to succeed is much more important than knowing what to do. Millions want to lose weight, but very few succeed. January and February of every year are littered with the abandoned goals of folks who started out with enthusiasm but ran out of gas. Knowing the steps to take is not the problem. Cultivating the ability to actually do them is where most of the work lies.

Your level of personal growth and development determines your level of performance and success in every area of your life. It determines the extent to which you utilize your God-given potential. Underutilized potential is a direct result of inadequate personal growth and development. Investing in yourself yields dividends in every facet of your life—business and career, family, money and investments, health and fitness, spiritual development and inner peace, social and community... It helps you discover who you are, what you are about, what you want, and how to get it. The impact of continuous personal growth is phenomenal.

To achieve what you have not achieved before, you must be who you have not been before. Who you are today produced the results you are seeing today. To get bigger results, you need a new you, a bigger you.

The starting point in your journey to greatness is to work on you. When you become great, doing great things follows naturally. As you grow as a person, you begin to achieve the things that were hitherto mission impossible, like sticking to an exercise, writing, reading, or savings routine, or anything you need to do to move to the next level. The more you grow, the easier it becomes.

MY STORY

I studied mechanical engineering in the mid 1980s with an eye on the oil sector because that was where the money was. Oil workers were royalty then. However, my passions were writing and building people and businesses. I also loved the outdoors, nature, and agriculture. Most of all I wanted a carefree life. I am not good at staying in boxes and climbing ladders. I prefer building ladders for others to climb.

I was a good engineer and breadwinner, but on the inside I was frustrated. I was not adept in corporate politics and found myself often cleaning up messes created by others who *were* good at climbing ladders. If I'd had a choice, I would have called it a day, but I had a family to feed and bills to pay.

I still believed I had no choice until my defining moment in 2001, when it dawned on me that I did have a choice. I realized I could hold on to my job and go for my dreams. All I needed to do was start minding my own business. I have been doing so since then, and I have formed companies, sat on a board, and resumed writing.

I stumbled on the link between personal growth and financial freedom by accident. I discovered the more I immersed myself in personal growth and development literature, the more I grew as a person. The more I grew as a person, the more easily I achieved tasks I used to struggle with. I became more patient, weighed my words before speaking, looked at issues from a long-term perspective, resumed exercising, read four books a month, and turned my car into a mobile success university. I discovered that rather than struggle with formulas and how-to's, I got better and more sustainable results by working on myself.

Looking back I restrain myself from calling my first ten to fifteen working years *the wasted years*. I feel sad whenever I think about how much time I frittered away rather than minding my own business. The time I lost to TV addiction, aimless gossip, and socializing led to a life devoid of dreams and purpose. I have virtually nothing to show for that time. If I had used it to build businesses, write books, develop myself, and so on, I would be much farther down the road than I am now. My consolation is that going through that experience made me the person I am now. I have been there, done that, and I know how it feels to have lost your way.

MAKE EVERYDAY COUNT

Yesterday is gone, but you can make the most of today. You can take back your dreams from where you abandoned them. You can start minding your own business. Nobody will do it for you.

Start by cutting out or reducing activities that do not move you toward your goals. You have a limited time on this planet. If you fritter it away, you can never get it back. Invest your time in things that will enrich you and others and leave lasting dividends.

Your clock is ticking. Make every hour count. Look at each day as capital that should bring returns and bring you closer to your most important goals. If it doesn't, then that is wasted time.

Put more effort into developing yourself than you put into your job. You have to assume the position of CEO of your life. Sack circumstances and take the driver's seat. Decide where you want to go and steer your life in that direction. It's your life, after all. Nobody else can live it for you.

IN SUMMARY

You are the CEO of your life and have ultimate responsibility for how it turns out. You have no one else to blame if you have no goals—or if you have goals but fail to achieve them. Take responsibility for your life and start minding your own business:

- Invest your time, don't just spend it.
- Don't be a spectator in life. Be an actor.
- Cut out or drastically reduce time-wasting activities like TV, games, browsing the Internet (especially social media), socializing and gossiping, etc. Invest that time in reading and learning for personal growth and development.
- Develop goals in every area of your life and pursue them. End each year better than how you started it in every area of your life.
- Go for your dreams.

12

MAKE YOUR TALENT PAY

When you are not practicing, someone somewhere is. And when the two of you meet, given roughly equal ability, he will win.

—Ed Macauley

We all have talents. No one is talentless.

Talent: *any natural or special gift; special aptitude or ability; eminent ability short of genius.*

In short talent is something you are naturally good at. It is inbuilt; you did not have to create it. That's part of who you are.

There is definitely something you are good at—something you can do well; your area of strength. Thinking you're not good at anything is false humility, an expression of low self-esteem and self-worth, and a disrespect to your person and your creator. It is an excuse for mediocrity.

Your talent has a lot to do with the reason you were born; it's what you have to offer the world to make it a better place.

131

It's your job to discover your talent and develop it to the point that you can start making meaningful contributions to society and the world at large. If you take your talent in its raw form and polish it till you become an expert, you will be rewarded beyond your wildest imagination.

The sad reality is that most people function in jobs outside where their talents lie. Most accept job offers based on remuneration, benefits, positions, and, in some instances, geographical location. Very few people make career decisions based primarily on the job's fit with their natural talents, passions, goals, and dreams.

Often we find our talents do not bring the quickest returns income-wise. Taking paid employment brings instant rewards by way of monthly pay, which allows us to get on with our lives. Becoming very good at your talent and making a living from it looks like a risky undertaking—something to attempt after retirement.

MAKING MONEY DOING WHAT YOU LOVE

The best place to be is where work, talent, and passion meet. The best returns on effort in the long term happen when you stay in the place of your strength, doing what you were born to do.

Make your talent pay. Start working on it and take it to the next level. Become very good at it at and turn it into a business or a vehicle for public good. You can work on your talent on a part-time basis and get better at it. You will reach a level where it will start making money. Some people refer to this as *the wealth zone*. Stretch your talent until you become an expert or genius and you're at the top of your game. Wealth and fame will soon become your everyday reality.

You are multitalented. You may be aware of this from the start or become aware down the line as you develop the one talent you know. Attempting to develop all your talents in one go will lead to a diffusion of focus. Take an inventory of your talents and focus on your area of greatest strength or where your passion lies as a start.

Your talent is given to you by God as raw material to accomplish your purpose. It is like a seed. You must plant it and nurture it and water it until it grows and blooms. That is your role in the equation. It will not happen without your effort.

If you take a close look at a celebrity or anyone on top of his or her game, you will find a common theme: they all became very good and what they were good at. They remained in their places of strength to become the best they could be. They followed their dreams. They moved from good to better and ultimately to the best. Financial freedom is not far away from where dreams come true.

IT TAKES HARD WORK TO BE THE BEST

Being the best will cost you. It does not come free. To attain greatness you must invest in developing your talent.

As Thomas Edison said, "Genius is ninety percent perspiration and ten percent inspiration". You have to work hard to attain your fullest potential. The best in every field is not always the most talented but the most hardworking. The secret is in constant practice. Build self-discipline, focus, persistence, eagerness to learn, and other success habits. Do whatever it takes to bring out the best in you. A coach will tell you the best players in the world stay behind to practice long after their colleagues have left the training pitch.

*When I played with Michael Jordan on the Olympic
team, there was a huge gap between his ability and
the ability of other players on that team. But what
impressed me was that he was always the first on the
floor and the last one to leave.*

—Steve Alford

Hard work is the differentiator. According to Malcolm
Gladwell in *Outliers*, you need to put in 10,000 hours of practice to attain excellence or become a genius. This is just a ball-
park figure. The underlying fact is that you have to work at it
until you become the best you can be. Attaining your utmost
potential does not happen automatically.

*I do not know anyone who has gotten to the top
without hard work. That is the recipe. It will not always
get you to the top, but it will get you pretty near.*

—Margaret Thatcher

Buy books on the area of your talent, study the masters,
and get a good mentor if possible. Practice, rehearse, practice
again and again—just do it! You perfect your act in the practice
arena. When it comes to doing the real thing, it will feel as if
you are still practicing. If you slouch on a couch and expect a
miracle, you will wait forever.

FIND YOUR GROOVE

Finding what you are good at is not rocket science. All you
need to do is be true to yourself and locate where your passion lies—where work seems like play. If you are clueless,
you may need to take a walk back down memory lane to your
childhood days, when you believed everything was possible.

Think about all the compliments you received. What did you do to earn them? That may be the key to locating what you're good at. Also ask authority figures in your life (parents, etc.) or trusted friends. They can point the way to what you're good at.

Celebrities, stars, billionaires, and other successful people are everyday men and women who took their talents and made fortunes out of them. J.K. Rowling was a single mother on welfare who became a billionaire by doing what she loves best—writing. She created Harry Potter and the rest, as they say, is history. All you need to do is to take your talents and dreams seriously and work on them. When you pay the full price, you will obtain the prize.

> *Don't give up too soon. Not even if well meaning*
> *parents, relatives, friends and colleagues tell you to get a*
> *"real job". Your dreams are your real job.*
> —JOYCE SPIZER

Show respect to what you have. Take it seriously and it will reward you. Whatever you despise will not confer any benefits on you.

Your talents hold the key to your financial freedom. Make your talents pay and you will be rewarded beyond your wildest imagination.

MY STORY

Prior to getting sucked into the rat race, my dream was to write, paint, own a business, and travel around the world and experience new cultures. As a youth I loved writing and the make-believe world of books. I was fascinated by words and their power to transport me from reality to another world.

I wrote my first book at age seventeen and my second at nineteen. My first manuscript was returned twice by publishers. My parents told me to get back to reality and get a university degree so I could get a real job. I came from an academic family. My parents took pride in the fact that they raised nine graduates with nineteen degrees between them. We had no family history of entrepreneurs or folks who followed their dreams and made it big. The closest anyone came to making it big was getting a good job.

I wanted to please my parents. I wanted to make them proud of me. Although my heart yearned for freedom, I decided playtime was over. It was time to grow up and face reality. I threw away my manuscripts and applied to a mechanical engineering program at the University of Benin in Nigeria. I gave up my dreams to become a writer, a painter, and an entrepreneur and became an engineer instead. I gave up writing, reading, painting, and dreaming.

When I resumed minding my own business, my dreams started to come alive once more. The first to return was my desire to become an entrepreneur. I started an online directory that blossomed into an information portal that has grown into a company with ten employees and counting. I tried my hand on other things and resumed writing. If you're reading this, it means my dreams of becoming a published author finally came to pass.

My desire to become a good writer has unveiled a talent I never knew I possessed: public speaking. I am still honing both skills and have started making money from them. It's still early, but the success I have achieved so far has given me confidence that my goals and dreams as a writer and public speaker will surely be accomplished. It's only a matter of time—after I have paid the full price.

IN SUMMARY

You have a talent. It's your job to discover what it is. Keep searching till you discover it, then commit to developing it to its fullest potential. Commit to paying the full price.

- Hard work separates the best from the average. Get to work honing your skills and talents.
- Practice, rehearse, practice again and again till you attain expertise.
- When you are among the best at what you do best, you will be among the top earners.
- Find your passion and follow your heart.
- Don't abandon your dreams for a "real" job. Your dreams are your real job.

13

DEVELOP MULTIPLE STREAMS OF INCOME

The trouble with the rat race is that even if you win,
you're still a rat.

—LILY TOMLIN

Depending on one source of income is an Industrial Age idea whose time has passed. Back then your job, income, and benefits were guaranteed. Gratuity and income were certain. You could stay with one company all your working life and be rewarded based on tenure and loyalty.

That world no longer exists. Some companies still run defined benefit plans, but they are a species approaching extinction. The rules of the game have changed and the marketplace has become global and borderless. Jobs get outsourced, and employers with huge pension overhangs get outplayed by sleeker competitors without such baggage. Employers no longer take care of you when you leave. You're on your own.

To mitigate these risks, you need multiple streams of income. When you depend on one source only, you operate in the Information Age with an Industrial Age mind-set. Your life revolves around your job. If your salary gets delayed, your finances go into crisis mode and you're at the risk of a financial meltdown. You live paycheck to paycheck. Your most frequently asked question is, "Have we been paid?"

Your salary determines your lifestyle. It determines where you live, what you can afford, and when you can pay for it. Major expenses are timed to coincide with paydays, which become the highlight of the month. Your life is wrapped around your salary. If your employer sneezes, you catch cold immediately. Your work is your life—literally.

In this situation being laid off from your job is your worst nightmare. If it happens your whole life goes into a tailspin. For many this results in their homes, cars, and sometimes furniture being repossessed. Some commit suicide rather than face life without a job. For corporate executives retirement means a reduction in their standard of living and a slide down the social strata. Some plunge from rich and upper middle class all the way down to poor. They bid goodbye to exotic holidays and luxury automobiles and hello to stipends and pensions.

If you want to attain financial freedom and ultimately become rich, you need multiple streams of income from diverse sources, especially the variety you do not have to labor for daily. On the average you should aim for at least three streams of income. The more the merrier.

When one stream dries up, you can live on the remaining two while getting another stream started. According to Robert Allen, the apostle of multiple streams of income, one of your yearly goals should be to decide how many streams you plan to add to your life in the course of that year. It does not mean taking a second job. Having one job is stressful enough. It means leveraging other types of income.

TYPES OF INCOME

There are three types of income:

1. **EARNED INCOME**: Here you exchange your time (your life, really) for money. Your day job falls into this category.
2. **PORTFOLIO INCOME**: This refers to income from paper assets like stocks, fixed deposits, bonds, treasury bills, etc. It also refers to income from businesses you own.
3. **PASSIVE INCOME**: This refers to cash flow from real estate investment and intellectual property like music, books, inventions, patents, etc.

Passive and portfolio income are the playground of the rich while the poor and middle class focus on earned income.

There are no right and wrong answers when it comes to what income class to focus on. Who you are and where you're going determine that. If you want to achieve financial freedom, exit the rat race, and live your dreams, focus more on portfolio and passive income. The beauty of this class is that you labor once and get paid forever through royalties from your intellectual property. All you need to do is create or acquire more assets that generate perpetual income. The result is that your income stream keeps increasing even when you stop working.

This does not happen with pensions. The value of your pension keeps going down, in effect making you poorer and poorer. With a vanishing pension you work and get paid—that's it. To earn the next income, you have to work again. The moment you stop working, you stop earning. The shelf life of your labor is one month. This is a very hard way to earn money.

OPEN YOUR MIND TO POSSIBILITIES

What you need is a mind-set adjustment and to brainstorm business ideas based on your environment. There are endless possibilities. Open your mind to see them. Start a business or invest in an existing business, real estate, etc. Use your talents and the opportunities around you to create multiple streams of income.

Developing multiple streams of income does not mean pursuing multiple opportunities at once. Stay with one stream at a time and grow it to the point where it becomes self-sustaining, requiring minimal input from you, before you start on the next. After you've put a system in place for running the business, most of the work is done. Hire an employee to carry on while you supervise to ensure the vision and business plan are being adhered to. If you are still an employee, focus on business ideas that will not distract you from performing your duties. Look for something you can work on during your spare time outside of work.

> *If you chase two rabbits, both will escape.*
> —PROVERB

Starting an Internet-based business is cheap and easy if you are willing to pay the price to learn. Any line of business can be conducted online, giving you immediate access to the global marketplace.

Social media has made marketing yourself and your products or services as simple as ABC. You no longer need to own a website to have a web presence. You can stay in your room with your laptop and develop multiple streams of income rather than squander endless hours watching TV.

You can turn each of your talents or hobbies into a stream of income, or spin off many streams from one talent alone, taking it to different dimensions or formats.

Whatever income class you choose, if you desire financial freedom rather than living from hand to mouth, develop multiple streams of income, so you do not remain at the mercy of one income source.

MY STORY

I started my journey to multiple streams of income by investing in stocks and money market instruments and starting an online business. As I shared earlier, I started with an online directory that is now a known online brand in Nigeria. I resumed my writing career by starting a website on financial freedom and later converted it to a blog. My experience in running the blog is what inspired me to write this book.

Publishing this book, coupled with my public speaking, will spin off other income streams like audio products, seminars, coaching, etc. This is just one aspect of what I do. The opportunities are limitless.

When I started opening my mind, I was overwhelmed by opportunities. I fell into the trap of attempting too much too soon but came to realize that attempting many things at the same time slows me down and lowers the quality of my output. I had to learn to focus on one stream of income at a time.

IN SUMMARY

Depending on a single source of income is risky in the Information Age. In an era of rapid changes, job security is a myth and each individual is responsible for taking his financial destiny into his own hands. You can no longer depend on your employer to take care of you for the rest of your life. In this era of mergers and corporate takeovers, it is foolhardy to assume the company will even be around well into your old age.

- Make a quality decision to stop living paycheck to paycheck.
- Hold on to your day job and use your spare time profitably, to develop multiple streams of income.
- Develop your talent, follow your passion, and turn your hobby into a business.
- You are multitalented. As you make good use of one talent, others become obvious.
- Become familiar with the three types of income – earned, portfolio and passive income. Determine which ones work best for you based on your financial goals.
- Keep adding new streams of income each year.
- Have an open mind and you will begin to see opportunities all around you.
- Develop one stream before you start on another.

14

TAKE BABY STEPS

The secret of getting ahead is getting started.
The secret of getting started is breaking your complex
overwhelming tasks into small manageable tasks, and
then starting on the first one.

—Mark Twain

It's easy to feel overwhelmed by the transformation that needs to happen to attain financial freedom. But remember everything big starts small. A journey of a thousand miles begins with one step, according to a Chinese proverb. That step is within your reach today. Forget about how far you need to go. It doesn't matter. Just take one step. The length of the stride is not an issue. As you start moving and gaining momentum, the other steps will follow.

If you can't fly, then run. If you can't run, then walk. If you
can't walk, then crawl. But whatever you do, you have to
keep moving forward.

—Martin Luther King Jr.

Take baby steps.
Take it step by step.
Take it every day.
Take it all the way.

If you're headed in the right direction, you'll definitely get to your destination. It's simply a matter of time.

MAKE "ONE OF THESE DAYS" TODAY

It's important to know where you're going, but to get there you must focus on what you can do today to make tomorrow happen. No matter how beautiful your goals and dreams are, if you do not take the requisite actions today, you're only daydreaming.

The key word is *today*. Don't wait until tomorrow. Take baby steps and keep moving. Don't stop. Don't wait. Keep going. Tomorrow is a myth. All you will always have is a continuous string of todays. What you don't do today will come to haunt you in the days ahead. Procrastination is a thief of destiny. The beauty of taking baby steps is that you can do it right now. The moment you make up your mind, act immediately. Do not let that moment pass. Do it now!

KEEP IT WITHIN YOUR STRIDE

If you overreach and stumble on the first step, you will become discouraged and may discontinue the journey. This is why it's important to take baby steps and increase gradually as you get comfortable with the length of your stride. If you're a couch potato starting an exercise regimen, you'll be advised to take it slow and steady, gradually increasing the duration and intensity of the routine. This is called *progressive overload*. If you attempt to show how motivated you are by running a marathon on day one, you'll end up in an emergency room. You have to step out of your comfort zone gently.

Your first step should be within your stride. It should be something you can do right now, not later. You have to start right where you are and the step must be doable now. If you earn $30,000 per annum and plan to save $50,000 per annum, it's not going to happen. However, in two or three years you could succeed in bringing onboard new streams of income or tripling your salary. Then saving $50,000 per annum becomes realistic.

It's very important to stay motivated along the journey, and nothing motivates more than tasks accomplished. They make you feel good, increase your confidence in achieving the next task, and boost your self-esteem. It's a positive cycle. Each step reinforces the next. Each success sets the stage for the next. It's important that you believe you can stay on top of your game—and do it. This belief becomes stronger as you actually achieve the next step and get closer to the main goal.

KEEP ON KEEPING ON

When taking baby steps, you may not get it right all the time. You may stumble and fall. That's okay and is to be expected. The issue is rising each time. When you stumble find out what went wrong, correct it, learn the lessons, and move on. If you overreached, reduce your stride accordingly and keep moving.

Start with baby steps and gradually increase your stride as you become better at it. You can be idealistic when setting your goal, but be realistic when setting the timeframe to achieve it. More often than not, it takes longer to achieve a goal than we first anticipate. The issue is not how long it takes but that it is achieved.

As you start on your journey, you can adjust timelines based on current realities. It's critical that the next step is achievable, as each step takes you closer to the goal. As you go along, your confidence and comfort level rises, and you become more audacious and stretch further.

Taking baby steps is not an excuse to linger around your comfort zone. Each successful step should take you farther away from it and closer to the overall goal. However, you have to be comfortable where you are before you can be bold enough to stretch further. This means creating many mini comfort zones along the way. When you reach a certain height, that becomes your new reality—but may become a new comfort zone if you linger too long.

Taking baby steps does not mean it's okay to settle on a new high. You need to keep moving, keep attaining new milestones along the path to your overall goal. Moving on is a lifelong activity. After achieving your goal and savoring the flush of victory, you have to set new goals and keep moving again.

> *The biggest goal can be accomplished if you just*
> *break it down into small enough steps.*
> —Henry Ford

What is your baby step?

That's a question only you can answer. Everyone is different, and what's comfortable to one can be a real stretch to another. For many it's reading another book. Adding to their body of knowledge until they get to the place where they feel comfortable enough to take action.

You have to determine the size of your baby steps based on where you are and what you're comfortable with. Choose a step you can commit to and achieve right now. At the end of the day, it's not how long your step is but that you take it in the first place. Then keep going one step at a time, one day at a time, till you cross the finish line.

MY STORY

I am truly amazed how far I have come from when I was a remote control wielding coach potato and TV addict. I did not make a sudden dash to where I am. In the beginning I felt sad about the years I had wasted on aimless living and attempted to make up for lost time by doing too much too soon. I tried to make progress in every area of my life where I identified a gap. I noticed after setting a goal and commencing action on it I soon lost steam. I set aggressive savings targets for myself, and after two months of putting in a valiant effort, I fell back to my old ways. I had similar experiences with exercise, writing, and other areas I needed to improve.

Apart from taking on too many things at the same time, I had unrealistic expectations with respect to the timelines for achieving my goals. I had to shift dates as I missed self-imposed deadlines—more than once in some instances.

As I learned to focus, take baby steps, and remain consistent, I began to gather momentum. One key area that paid off handsomely is my investment in personal growth and development. This gave me the drive to follow through, which is critical in goal achievement. It has been a very exciting journey. The fact that I have come so far gives me confidence that I will cross the finish line of all my goals.

IN SUMMARY

Decide on a key area where you need to take immediate action and focus on it. Start small. Take baby steps. Sustainability of your effort is of paramount importance. Take a step you are comfortable with. Just by all means start.

- Take action immediately while you're in the mood to get going. Don't wait until your enthusiasm grows cold and the zeal diminishes. Don't procrastinate.
- Keep on keeping on. Take steps you're comfortable with, whether it's crawling, walking, running, or flying. Just keep moving. Keep the momentum going. Do not lose steam.
- You can take bigger strides as you gradually step up your game.
- Remain focused and consistent. Achieving goals is a marathon, not a hundred-meter dash.

15

INSURE YOUR ASSETS

I detest life-insurance agents; they always argue that
I shall someday die, which is not so.
—Stephen Leacock

The common thread in your journey to financial freedom is control—being in the driver's seat of your finances. It means being the one to determine outcomes rather than give in to forces outside of your control.

You can determine how events impact you with the actions you take before they happen. In terms of risk, do this by insuring your assets. You may not be able to stop the event or accident from happening, but you can control the impact it has on your finances so that heads or tails, you'll still be in the game and on track to achieve your financial goals.

"INDECENT" EXPOSURE

Exposing your assets to possible loss is known as *investing naked* or *taking a naked position*. If fire or a natural disaster levels your property, you have taken a direct hit. If your property was fully insured, your insurers will restore you to where you were financially before the disaster hit. This is called *indemnity*.

Take insurance policies out on all your valuables, especially assets. This ranges from your home and its contents to your business and its assets (computers, furniture, etc.) to your life. A fire or burglary can shut down your business for weeks if you lose your computers or servers and you have no sufficient cash or credit to replace them immediately.

The interesting thing about insurance is that you have to take a policy when you don't need one. The moment the event happens and you need insurance, if you don't have it, it's too late. Protecting your assets also involves having a backup of all your critical data, preferably in a different location. You want to be back in business as soon as possible after an incident.

Having an insurance policy works out cheaper in the long run than taking a naked position and praying nothing happens. If an event like a fire, a natural disaster, or a burglary happens to you, your previous gains may not cover your loss. Lack of insurance has wiped out some businesses. Don't take that risk. It isn't worth it.

Have a backup plan for unforeseen circumstances. Your health and your life are assets. Insure them. Same with goods in transit. There is an insurance policy to cover any foreseeable risk scenario. Do not cut corners. Do not allow an unexpected event to blindside you. Retain control of possible outcomes. Remain on top of your game by taking a covered position. A naked position leaves you exposed and not in control. It's too risky. It's gambling.

PROTECT YOUR INVESTMENTS

Protecting your assets includes taking a covered position when you invest. You must have entry and exit strategies anytime you invest. Don't just dive in, hope, and pray. Don't just react to the market. Proactively plan ahead and get out when your exit conditions have been met.

Take the stock market for example. Most people know how to make money in a bull market but panic when the bears take over. A savvy investor knows how to make money in all market situations. He knows how to hedge against loss. He takes a long position to take profits in a bull run and a short position to make money when the market dips. He cut his losses in the event of a crash. He does not become greedy and pray for a permanent bull run. He locks in his profits and exits as the market heads back down. No surprises. Heads or tails he wins.

Using longs and shorts also works in options trading, where the sophisticated investor can win in up and down markets, and forex trading. An experienced trader locks in his position and sets his stop-loss and take-profit positions. By doing this he determines the outcome of each trade, win or lose. He has an entry and exit strategy for each trading day and determines how much profit he makes and how much loss he is willing to take. In summary he takes a covered position. He does not expose his investment to market volatility. Inexperienced traders can get wiped out by wide market swings.

It doesn't makes sense to proceed based on the hope that nothing wrong will happen—or to live under the shadow of fear that something very well might.

GET A GOOD INSURANCE BROKER

A good insurance broker should be a member of your team. Like other members of your team, he should come highly recommended by trusted sources, after having done your due diligence and asking the right questions. The insurance industry has an array of products that offer both insurance cover and growth. A good broker will advise you on investing through insurance products and get you the best deal on those products since he understands the market, what different insurance companies offer, and what works best for you based on your investment objectives.

An insurance salesman works for a particular insurance company and will attempt to sell you products from the stable of that company. An insurance broker deals with different insurance companies, hence he has a broader view of what's on offer in the market and what products to offer to clients based on their investment needs and circumstances.

THE COST OF DOING BUSINESS

A lot of small business owners and individuals feel taking insurance is a waste of money, as the risk they are insured against may not occur. But insurance is part of the cost of doing business and ultimately gets passed on to the consumer. It's part of your overhead costs.

For individuals insurance premiums should be factored into buying decisions to determine affordability. If you plan to buy your dream luxury car and cannot afford the annual insurance, then you truly cannot afford that car. Avoiding insurance exposes your to unnecessary risk and, in some instances, breaks the law.

Some classes of insurance are mandatory. However, you do not need the law or government to club you on the head for you to realize the need to insure your valuables. Do not cut corners when it comes to insurance. Do not expose yourself. Cover yourself. Get insured.

MY STORY

My business premises were burgled once but nothing significant was stolen, so there was no need to contact the insurance company. I have a couple of friends whose businesses lost assets due to burglary and accidents. They had no insurance coverage. One was able to replace the stolen items, though it took a while and adversely affected his returns over that year. The other friend could not get back on his feet and the business ultimately folded. It was a very painful lesson.

When I got involved in a minor car crash in 2010 due to brake failure on my vehicle, the repair bill for both vehicles involved came to almost $4,000, which was picked up by my insurance company. If I'd had no insurance, the bill would have punched a giant hole in my budget and negatively impacted my financial goals for that year. Because I had an insurance policy, the only impacts the accident had on me were the dent in my driving record and the punch on the nose from the deployed airbag.

IN SUMMARY

Do not leave your assets exposed to risk. Insure your assets and investments. Do not leave outcomes to chance.

Have a plan for when things go right and when things go wrong. It's penny wise and pound foolish to hope and pray that nothing bad will happen to you. Sometimes bad things happen to good people. It's part of life.

- Plan for the unexpected. Don't wait until something unexpected happens to you.
- Have entry and exit strategies for every investment so you're not taken by surprise by market swings.
- Insurance is part of the cost of doing business. It's part of your business overhead. Do not cut corners.
- Get expert advice. Get a good insurance broker on your team.

16

PRACTICE ASSET ALLOCATION

The financial markets generally are unpredictable.
So that one has to have different scenarios...The idea
that you can actually predict what's going to happen
contradicts my way of looking at the market.
—GEORGE SOROS

Asset allocation is a very powerful yet simple tool you must use to protect your finances from inevitable storms that arise from market crashes, fear, greed, and impulsive investment decisions. Regardless what your financial goal is—to be secure, comfortable, or rich—you need a plan that can weather all storms to achieve it.

Asset allocation builds rings of defense around your finances so when the storms come, you will not take a direct hit and have to start all over again. With a solid financial base, you can reach your financial goals and dreams.

There are three investment plans, vehicles, or buckets to choose from. After spending below your means and paying yourself first, the money you save has to be allocated into one of these three:

1. Plan to be secure (or the financial security bucket)
2. Plan to be comfortable (or the growth bucket)
3. Plan to be rich (or the dream bucket)

For a solid financial foundation, the plan to be secure must come first, followed by the plan to be comfortable before you attempt to be rich. Financial security is the foundation upon which all the other goals build. If you attempt to be comfortable or rich without financial security, you're like the man who builds a house on sand. When the storms come, great shall be the fall of such a building. If you bypass the foundation and start on the building, what you have is an accident waiting to happen.

PLAN TO BE SECURE

This plan is for fixed-income investments, where returns are known and guaranteed. This includes interest income from savings, money market instruments like certificate of deposits or fixed deposits, bonds, treasury bills, etc. These are low-risk and low-return investments. Interest rates can vary from one to twenty percent depending on the country and economic conditions. This plan is not glamorous; in fact it's predictable and often boring. That's why many don't stick with it. You can take an excel spreadsheet and track your income one year ahead (if rates remain the same). However, this is where the miracle of compound interest holds sway. If you can leave your interest income to compound, you will be amazed what it will amount to over the years. It requires discipline and consistency to yield tangible results.

Typically this is where you place your emergency savings (two to six months of take-home pay), insurance investment products, etc. This plan protects you from unforeseen financial circumstances like job loss or a market crash. Since income is guaranteed, this plan provides security, hence the name. This means if the market crashes, you lose your job, or the business fails, you still have a home, your car, and money to meet your basic needs.

Ideally you want to grow this plan until you attain financial independence, which means income from this plan is enough to cover your monthly expenses so you don't have to work again for the rest of your life if you choose not to. When you get to this point, you keep on working because you want to, not because you have to. To achieve this you have to remain focused and be disciplined, and keep working the plan and reinvesting the interest for faster returns.

Unfortunately this plan or bucket is often left empty. This is what we raid to get money to place in higher risk investments that often backfire. Also we often leave it empty because we want to get higher returns from the other plans. Very few people have plans for security. Employees typically regard their jobs as their financial security, hence they hardly save, and when they manage to invest they go for growth investments for higher returns. This is why some people cling to jobs they hate. They have no safety nets. If they lose their jobs, the roof and walls come tumbling down because of a lack of solid foundation of financial security.

The few with plans to be secure often give in to the temptation of liquidating their plans anytime someone offers what looks like a very good deal with much higher returns. The original intent may be to borrow the funds and replace them at a later date. More often than not, the investment doesn't turn out as hoped or the money never gets replaced.

You need to determine upfront what fixed percentage will go into each plan no matter what.

PLAN TO BE COMFORTABLE

This is where we invest for greater returns or growth. This plan takes us beyond the level of security to making some good money. The risks and returns are higher. It involves investing in the stock market, real estate, futures, the commodity market, the forex market, and other markets. You can double the value of your portfolio in a short time. You can also lose your money. The return of your seed capital is not guaranteed.

The plan is to buy low and sell high. You need a good financial education to play at this level. Ideally it's better to start with the plan to be secure and build it up while acquiring financial education before attempting to invest. If you don't have a solid security plan in place, a crash of your growth plan can bring down your entire financial house, depending on the magnitude of the loss. In a margin loan scenario, you can go in with your money and walk away in debt.

Stick to your plan and avoid the temptation to rob Peter to pay Paul. If you do not have enough money, allow the deal to pass. That will give you time to clear your head and do proper due diligence.

PLAN TO BE RICH

This is the most romantic of all the plans, and most people are tempted to start here. Everybody wants to be rich or look rich, but most are not patient enough to pay the price in investment education before they plunge in. Often the fool and his money part ways here and for most it's back to square one, as the plans to be secure and comfortable are not in place to catch them. Some people have lost homes and cars because of one investment decision that went bad.

This plan involves investing in businesses (startups, venture capital, private placements, etc.), high leverage investment in real estate development using other people's money and other very high-risk and high-return investments. The returns here are fabulous. They can range from twenty-five percent to infinity. It's the stuff rags to riches stories and fairy tales are made of.

Due to expected high returns, there is often a strong pull to risk it all and win big. The flip side is risking it all and losing it all. When greed kicks in, you're ready to risk everything, including wiping out the two other plans to raise the money.

It's too dangerous to risk everything on one investment. Many have sad tales to tell of such misadventures. Stick to the plan.

MY STORY

Although I first learned of this concept from the Rich Dad series, I did not have the discipline at the early stages of my journey to stick to the plan. I often raided my other plans when I wanted to fund my real estate transactions. Due to my inconsistency, my plan to be secure did not generate enough cash flow to cover my living expenses. I was back to square one after each real estate transaction.

The direct consequence of not meeting my target for financial independence was that I remained dependent on my job for financial security. I kept shifting the goalpost for attaining financial independence and ultimately quitting my job. While watching a DVD by Anthony Robbins on financial freedom I realized that though I was familiar with asset allocation at the intellectual level, there was no emotional connection that moved me to take action. It dawned on me that I'd been sabotaging my efforts to attain financial independence. I had to return to the basics and build my financial foundation afresh.

IN SUMMARY

Building a strong financial foundation to attain financial freedom requires having all the plans in place in the right sequence. You have to do first things first. While it's possible to win in the short term by robbing your fixed-income assets to invest in speculative investment, you cannot go the distance. Experienced gamblers in Las Vegas will tell you winning big is the worst thing that can happen. Greedy for more, you will raise the stakes and risk it all for a bigger win. When greed kicks in, you're a goner. However, you rarely go wrong when you stick to the plan.

- Decide upfront how you want to allocate your assets. Most of your funds should go to your plan to be secure. That is your financial foundation.
- Be consistent every month. Pay yourself first and remit the funds to the right plan automatically.
- Your goal should be to attain financial independence, which means generating enough income from your fixed-income assets to cover your living expenses.
- Do not borrow funds from your plan to be secure to invest in other plans. Work based on your asset allocation plan, allow each plan to attain critical mass through consistent monthly allocation of funds from your savings.
- Upon attainment of financial independence, you can choose to reduce the allocation to your plan to be secure and focus more on your plans to be comfortable and rich. Become an investor before investing.

17

PLAN YOUR ESTATE

Expect the best, plan for the worst, and prepare to be surprised.

—DENIS WAITLEY

The world is like a stage, and the time will come when you'll have to take your final bow. You can determine what happens to your estate when you're gone by planning properly.

You can continue to do good, impact lives, and take care of your loved ones long after you're gone. It doesn't make sense to work long and hard to build your estate and then leave it to the government, predators, cultural idiosyncrasies, or feuding siblings to decide how it's administered. Horror stories abound wherein the wife and young children of the deceased are stripped of their inheritances and thrown out on the streets because the man died intestate—without a will or a trust to instruct how his possessions should be divided.

If a person or estate is intestate, then the disposition of the possessions are handled by probate law. A court proceeding will determine how they will be divided among heirs, creditors, and anyone else who has a rightful claim to them.

Because this process is expensive and lengthy and can sometimes get ugly (especially with unscrupulous descendants, relatives, or con artists), dying intestate is something to avoid. Love demands that you make provisions for the upkeep of your loved ones and possible propagation of your dreams long after you have gone. Your dreams should not die with you. The baton should be handed down from generation to generation. Success without a successor is failure. Many businesses do not transcend generations. Most die with their founders.

WRITE YOUR WILL

Writing a will, or setting up a living trust before death, ensures the process of the transfer of possessions will happen inexpensively, quickly, and without abuse or rancor among family members. In ensures things will go according to plan after you're gone. It means that even at death you make things happen rather than allow external circumstances to determine the outcome of your efforts. You get to decide who gets what, who is in charge of what, and what happens after you are gone.

It's difficult for most of us to come to terms with our mortality. It can be difficult to contemplate that a day will come when we will leave behind our loved ones and everything we labored long and hard for. Love demands we ensure our loved ones are well provided for after we are gone. It is irresponsible to allow them to clean up the mess we left by not putting our estate and finances in order.

Thinking an unexpected death can only happen to others is hiding your head in the sand. It takes courage to come to terms with your mortality and plan accordingly. Planning your estate empowers you. It helps you know that nothing will be left to chance. You won't leave your estate in a naked and powerless position. If anything happens to you, all your bases will be covered to the best of your ability.

I know the feeling because I have walked that path. Making your will gives you a better perspective of how your dreams will interface with the next generation. Are you going to hand over your business to your son or daughter? Or would you rather take your company public and build an institution that does not depend on your family for continuity? Your will makes you see beyond your time here on earth. It makes you realize you are not here for yourself and your family only.

You are a piece in a giant jigsaw puzzle. What happens when you're gone? How do you want to be remembered? What do you want written on your tombstone? Alfred Nobel died in 1896, but his estate lives on more than 115 years later, doing good worldwide and advancing the causes of science, arts, medicine, peace, and literature through the Nobel Prize.

SOMETIMES TOMORROW NEVER COMES

When it comes to planning your estate, it's easy to feel you have all the time in the world. You may believe you will live to a ripe old age with time enough to gather your great-grand-children to your bedside to say your final farewell. I wish that for you too. But whatever your beliefs, you have no control over when you will pass. Your life is not in your hands, so you must put your house and affairs in order. Live as if you have a few weeks to go, and plan as if you will live forever. Whatever happens, you need to be ready for your final curtain call.

People who die young had no idea they would leave the planet early. People who die in automobile accidents do not get a week's notice. I come to terms with my mortality over and over again whenever I lose someone close to me. Over the years, I have lost close peers and colleagues, some in their twenties. We plan for tomorrow but sometimes tomorrow never comes. Today is a gift, and we need to make the most of it.

There is no better time than today to call your attorney (or hire one) and put a will in place. Through your will you determine where your assets or estate goes when you are gone. A will is a legal document protected by the state. You can update it at intervals as your assets portfolio grows.

Financial freedom is about control. The moment you lose control, you lose the plot. You have to make things happen rather than let things happen to you. You cannot control tomorrow. But you can influence it by taking the right steps today.

IN SUMMARY
Having worked hard to take control of your finances and build your asset portfolio and estate, you need to be able to pass them on. Retain control of this process rather than having outsiders do it for you. You are the best person to make provisions for your loved ones after you have moved on.

- Start planning your estate. Determine how it will be administered and what good you will continue to do after you're gone.
- If you own a business, develop an exit strategy if you have not done so already. If you plan to pass on the business to your children, have a succession plan.
- Prepare your will immediately. Do not delay it any longer.

- Get legal advice. Have a lawyer review, offer advice on, format, and formalize your will. Review your options and make informed decisions.
- Planning for the future makes you feel more confident and gives you clarity. Having a will does not mean you are wishing for death. As a matter of fact, it makes you face the future with more boldness, knowing you are fully prepared.

18

GIVE BACK TO SOCIETY

Ignoring your passion is like dying a slow death...
Passion whispers to you through your feelings, beckoning
you toward your highest good. Pay attention to what
makes you feel energized, connected, stimulated—what
gives you your juice. Do what you love, give it back in
the form of service, and you will do more than succeed.
You will triumph.

—OPRAH WINFREY

Your journey to financial freedom culminates in the giving back phase. When you attain financial freedom and independence, it will dawn on you that this is not about money. Looking back you will see that you received a lot along the way and met people who changed your life forever. Now it's payback time—time to give back to society and make the world a better place because you came, leaving indelible footprints in the sands of time.

Our purpose on earth is inextricably tied to giving of ourselves, touching lives, and making a difference for the good.

Life can be broadly divided into three phases:

1. Learning
2. Earning
3. Giving

The learning phase typically occurs between the ages of zero and twenty-five, a time we receive from others, discover who we are (hopefully), chose a vocation, and get an education. The earning phase typically occurs between the ages of twenty-five and fifty, a time we earn money. The giving phase typically happens in the fifties. This is, however, not cast in concrete, as we are always learning, some start earning earlier than others, and others start giving back in their twenties and thirties.

Financial freedom is not about making all the money we can and fulfilling all our childhood fantasies, as good as they are. It's much more than that. Money is a tool for doing good. We're meant to be conduits of blessings to others, to make their dreams come true. We are not lakes to trap and hold everything for ourselves. Think of the Dead Sea, which receives water but never gives and out—and ends up stinking.

The money that flows into our lives is not for us only but to bless those whose lives and destinies are linked to ours. We cannot live our lives fully if we do not give fully of ourselves and our substance to make others' dreams come true.

Do all the good you can, by all the means you can,
in all the ways you can, in all the places you can, at
all the times you can, to all the people you can, as long
as ever you can.
—JOHN WESLEY

If you look close enough, you'll see every God-given dream is beyond you; it has something to do with others. A teacher teaches not herself but others. A writer writes for others, a singer sings for others. A painter does not paint for himself. A surgeon does not operate on himself. We are not living for ourselves

OUR TRUE CLAIM TO IMMORTALITY

What constitutes success? She who has achieved success has lived well; laughed often and loved much; has gained the respect of little children; has filled her niche and accomplished her task; has left the world better than she found it; has always looked for the best in others and given the best she had.
—BESSIE ANDERSON STANLEY

Financial freedom is not about money. It is freedom from the control of money. We are not to be slaves to money but masters.

Giving back gives us control over greed and selfishness and connects us to a purpose beyond ourselves. Our true claim to immortality lies in the good we do for others, not the assets we accumulate, the money we make, or the monuments we build. Those can perish with time. Money is a consumable—a tool, not an asset to grab. It's meant to circulate and do good around the world. We have to give to others and spread joy.

In life there will always be those we look up to and those who look up to us. God answers prayers through people. We can be an answer to someone else's prayer.

Running after money is like chasing the wind. It grows wings and flies away. But as we give it away, it comes back to us. We spread joy, hope, and goodwill as we give to others. We inspire them to reach out for their dreams and give to others too. The good we do creates a ripple effect as it gets propagated cross the globe.

In an increasingly selfish world, givers make a difference and never lack. A company with tremendous goodwill through giving does not struggle in building an enduring brand. It has already won a place in the hearts of the people. The fastest way to riches is to discover a need and provide a solution to it. People are very willing to pay for such a service. Money should not be the motive for our service but a reward.

BE TRUE TO YOURSELF

It all comes back to our motives. We have to remain true to ourselves and at peace with our core values. Beyond the survival level, money achieves very little. The best things in life are free.

My dream is to set up a foundation that will feed orphans, send them to school, and provide tools and information to help make their dreams come true. It's still early, and I am still putting the paperwork together. I hope to start at home—in the Niger Delta in Nigeria, then go to Liberia, South Sudan, and other places around the globe where needs are great. To me it's an appointment with destiny. My desire is to see this foundation grow big in my lifetime and make a greater impact long after I'm gone.

Our success is not measured by how much we accumulate while on earth but how many lives we touch and how many people will miss us when we take the final bow.

Nothing satisfies like putting a smile in the face of the hopeless and bringing succor to the down and out. Nothing brings joy like making a difference in other people's lives and leaving the world better than it was when we met it.

This is the ultimate freedom.

EPILOGUE

Making the decision to go for financial freedom is one of the most important decisions you will ever make. The journey to financial freedom takes you down the path of financial education and personal growth and development and positively impacts every area of your life as you grow and evolve as a person.

To achieve what you have not achieved before, you have to become who you have not been before. Through continuous growth and improvement, your possibilities are limitless. The process of becoming is what makes the journey much more exciting than the destination itself.

In seeking financial freedom, I have found much more than financial freedom. I have embarked on a lifelong journey of learning and growth. I have grown as a person. I have become more knowledgeable, more confident, better equipped to deal with my weaknesses, fitter, a better husband and father, and more at peace with myself, and I have a greater connection to my purpose and God. I am still amazed by the all-around change I have experienced.

As I've traveled down this road, a lot of things have started to make sense. New doors have swung open and new people have come into my life as I've thought and acted differently. I have found myself and become an author, an entrepreneur, a mentor, a teacher, and a speaker. Sometimes I feel like Alice in Wonderland. That windy summer Sunday afternoon I gazed in anger and frustration at a clear London sky has become a distant memory.

Life is truly beautiful and nothing is impossible to he who believes. Ask and you shall receive; seek and you shall find; knock and the door shall be opened to you. I used to know this in my head from Sunday school, but now it has become my everyday reality. I feel grateful, awed, and emotional whenever I look back at where I started and how far I have come. What really blows me away is knowing that all my dreams are possible.

If a shy country boy with a massive dose of low self-esteem, more seen than heard, who spent his time after school daydreaming or babysitting his nieces and nephews can make it, I believe anybody can. There are no excuses whatsoever. If you believe you can long enough, soon you will. Your dream beckons. You have to reach out for it.

If you have come this far, I believe you have started your journey to financial independence. If you can commit to life-long learning and growth, the changes you desire to make happen will start to take place, starting with how you think. You are in for a makeover beyond your wildest imagination.

As you begin your journey, you will grow as a person and discover exciting new things about yourself—things you never thought yourself capable of. At the beginning your journey may be motivated by the desire to escape the rat race and achieve financial freedom. At the end you'll have found yourself. You'll get to know who you are and what you're about. Few things can be as rewarding.

EPILOGUE

We shall not cease from exploration, and the end of
all our exploring will be to arrive where we started and
know the place for the first time.

—T.S. ELIOT

By the time you cross the finish line, looking back you can see the journey was not about money but finding yourself, who you really are, and giving all you have to make the world a better place because you came.

I hope reading this book has changed your life the way writing it has changed mine. In trying to give, I have received much more. In seeking to teach, I have learned much more. In seeking to change lives, my life has changed forever. Indeed it is more blessed to give than to receive.

You can achieve anything you want if you need it enough to pay the full price upfront and in full. If you've come this far, you have what it takes to go for your dreams. Keep learning. Keep growing. Never give up. Dreams do come true. You can live yours.

Bon voyage and Godspeed, my friend!
Usiere Uko
March 2012

RECOMMENDED READING

No matter how busy you may think you are, you must find time for reading, or surrender yourself to self-chosen ignorance.

—CONFUCIUS

There are tons of excellent books on the subjects of personal finance, growth, and development. These are just a few to get you going. Start with at least one book a month.

1. *Rich Dad, Poor Dad:What the Rich Teach Kids About Money That the Poor and Middle Class Do Not!* by Robert Kiyosaki
2. *Rich Dad's Cashflow Quadrant: Rich Dad's Guide to Financial Freedom* by Robert Kiyosaki
3. *The Millionaire Next Door* by Thomas J Stanley and William Danko
4. *The Millionaire Mind:The Surprising Secrets of America's Wealth* by Thomas J Stanley
5. *The Richest Man in Babylon* by George S Clason
6. *The Rules of Wealth* by Richard Templar
7. *The Courage to Be Rich: Creating a Life of Material and Spiritual Abundance* by Suze Orman
8. *Multiple Streams of Income: How to Generate a Lifetime of Unlimited Wealth!* by Robert G. Allen

9. *Caught Between a Dream and a Job: How to Leave the 9-to 5 Behind and Step Into the Life You've Always Wanted* by Delatorro McNeal II
10. *The Strangest Secret* by Earl Nightingale
11. *Think and Grow Rich* by Napoleon Hill
12. *Live Your Dreams* by Les Brown
13. *Put Your Dream to The Test: 10 Questions to Help You See It and Seize It* by John C. Maxwell
14. *Make Today Count: The Secret of Your Success Is Determined by Your Daily Agenda* by John C. Maxwell
15. *The Power of Focus: How to Hit Your Business, Personal and Financial Targets With Absolute Certainty* by Jack Canfield, Mark Victor Hansen, and Les Hewitt
16. *The Success Principles: How to Get From Where You Are to Where You Want to Be* by Jack Canfield
17. *Focal Point: A Proven System to Simplify Your Life, Double Your Productivity and Achieve All Your Goals* by Brian Tracy
18. *Goals!: How to Get Everything You Want—Faster Than You Ever Thought Possible* by Brian Tracy
19. *No Excuses!: The Power of Self-Discipline* by Brian Tracy
20. *The Purpose-Driven Life: What on Earth Am I Here For?* by Rick Warren

ABOUT THE AUTHOR

Usiere Uko is an entrepreneur, a writer, and a speaker. A mechanical engineer with a career spanning twenty years in Nigeria's oil and gas industry, he commenced his journey to financial freedom in December 2001, when he first came across the *New York Times* best-selling book *Rich Dad, Poor Dad* by Robert Kiyosaki. He has since gone on to found NigeriaGalleria.Com, Nigeria's foremost information portal, and other startups in the ICT and real estate sectors. Through his personal journey to financial freedom, he has rediscovered and returned to his first love—writing—through which he hopes to inspire others to live their dreams.

Usiere retired from the Nigerian National Petroleum Corporation in 2007 and now lives Lagos, Nigeria. He is the author of the personal finance, investing, inspirational, and motivational blog www.financialfreedominspiration.com. He is happily married with two children.